101 Best Vegan Quinoa Recipes Cookbook

Alison Thompson

Table of Contents

http://www.101BestCookbooks.com/veganquinoa

Introduction

Thank you for purchasing this book about vegan quinoa recipes!

All attempt has been made to make sure these recipes are accurate and delicious! WARNING: Please be sure to read labels of pre manufactured foods to be sure they are vegan friendly. Also we are aware that there is some controversy as to whether or not yeast is vegan. We have included a few recipes using yeast. It is up to you to make a decision as to whether or not you will use the recipes with yeast.

Please note that the recipes below where compiled from different sources to give you one complete cookbook you can have with you in the kitchen. All recipes are in the public domain (copyright law prohibits copyrighting basic recipes, only commentary about the recipes falls under US copyright law). No copyright was infringed and the reader of this book may copy the recipes at their own pleasure and share with others! However the format of this book does fall under copyright protection and so this book itself can not be copied in it's entirety. **Please enjoy these Quinoa recipes and Happy Healthy Eating**!

Want to share your recipes and talk with other quinoa lovers? Go to **www.101BestCookbooks.com/veganquinoa**

Chapter 1 - Vegan Quinoa Breakfast

Warm and Nutty Cinnamon Quinoa Recipe

1 cup organic almond milk
1 cup water
1 cup organic quinoa, rinse quinoa
2 cups fresh blackberries, organic preferred
1/2 teaspoon ground cinnamon
1/3 cup chopped pecans, toasted*
4 teaspoons organic agave nectar

Combine almond milk, water and quinoa in a medium saucepan. Bring to a boil over high heat. Reduce heat to medium-low; cover and simmer 15 minutes or until most of the liquid is absorbed. Turn off heat; let stand covered 5 minutes. Stir in blackberries and cinnamon; transfer to four bowls and top with pecans. Drizzle 1 teaspoon agave nectar over each serving.

*While the quinoa cooks, roast the pecans in a 350F degree toaster oven for 5 to 6 minutes or in a dry skillet over medium heat for about 3 minute

Spicy Quinoa Breakfast Burrito

1/4 cups cooked quinoa
1/4 onion (chopped)
1/4 green pepper (chopped)
1 garlic clove (chopped)
1/4 medium tomato
cayenne pepper
paprika
fresh ground pepper
1/4 cup egg substitute
1 brown rice tortilla
1/4 avocado

Directions:

All ingredient amounts are approximate. Use what you feel is right.

Coat bottom of pan with oil, add quinoa, onion, pepper, and garlic.

Add spices to taste.

Cook until veggies are golden, stirring so that everything is completely coated in spices.

Add egg substitute, scramble until cooked.

In separate pan, heat tortilla until golden brown.

Put ingredients into tortilla, adding avocado. Fold into burrito, and enjoy!

Apple Cinnamon Breakfast Quinoa

1 small-medium apple
1/2 tbsp lemon juice
1 tsp ground cinnamon
1/4 cup water
1/2 tbsp agave nectar
1/4 cup uncooked quinoa

Core and cut the apple (leaving the skin on) into chunks. Place them in a blender with the lemon juice, cinnamon and water. Blend until smooth. Taste it, if it's not sweet enough add the agave and blend again.

Place the apple mixture and quinoa into a small pan over medium-high heat. Stir continuously until it begins to boils. Once it boils, cover and lower to a simmer. Simmer for 15-20 minutes. The quinoa will absorb the liquid and just begin to turn transparent with little visible rings. Remove from heat and serve

Milky Quinoa Breakfast Recipe

1 Apple
¼ cup quinoa
2 tbsp pecans
1/2 cup rice milk
2 tbsp flax seed

Directions

Cook Quinoa, chop apple, mix and serve. Try cinnamon, nutmeg or ginger for extra taste!

Crock Pot Quinoa Breakfast

1 1/2 cups quinoa, rinsed well
4 cups water
1 cup chopped dried fruit, unsulphered (any type or a mixture)
1/4 cup raisins
1/4 cup dates, chopped
1/2 teaspoon ground cinnamon
1/4 teaspoon ground coriander
1/4 cup chopped Brazil nuts (optional)

DIRECTIONS

Place all ingredients in a crock pot and turn on warm overnight or for 10 hours.

Add some soy milk if desired.

If you'd prefer making this in the morning, then simmer the quinoa in the water for 10 minutes and then add rest of ingredients and simmer for 5 more minutes until all liquid is absorbed.

Note: When done in a crock pot, if a crust develops around the edges, just dispose of that part. Quinoa is a grain which is a good source of iron, protein, and other nutrients. Be sure to rinse it well, using a small screen strainer, since some of the bitter coating may not have been removed during processing.

HOT QUINOA BREAKFAST CEREAL

1 c Quinoa
2 c Water
1/2c Apples -- thinly sliced
1/3c Raisins
1/2 tsp Cinnamon
Almond or Rice Milk
Agave Nectar or brown sugar

Rinse quinoa and add to water; bring to a boil.

Reduce heat; simmer for 5 minutes. Add apples,

Raisins and cinnamon; simmer until water is absorbed.

Serve with almond or rice milk and sweeten to taste with agave or brown sugar.

Breakfast Quinoa Ingredients

1/4 cup uncooked quinoa
2 Tbsp hemp seeds
1/2 cup unsweetened almond milk or fresh made almond milk
1 Tbsp raisins
1 med fresh peach
1/4 teaspoon vanilla extract
Stevia or agave nectar to sweeten

Rinse Quinoa and combine with almond milk and water.
Bring to a slow simmer, then

Cover and cook for about 15 minutes until the quinoa is tender.
Stir in the remaining ingredients and

Place in food processor or blender and puree slightly.
Ready to eat.

Creamy Coconut Mango Quinoa Breakfast

1/2 cup rinsed quinoa
1 mango, peeled and cubed
1 cup coconut milk
1 tablespoon cinnamon
1 teaspoon agave nectar

Warm coconut milk and cinnamon in a medium pot. Add quinoa and cook, covered, for about 25 minutes on low medium heat.

Before the quinoa absorbs all the coconut milk, add the mango and cook for 5 more minutes until it is fluffy. Drizzle agave nectar on top and eat

Fruited Breakfast Quinoa

1/2 cup rinsed quinoa
1-1/2 cups vanilla rice milk
2 tablespoons raisins
1 cup chopped fresh or canned apricots
1/4 teaspoon vanilla extract

To thoroughly rinse quinoa, cover it with water in a mixing bowl, then rub it between the palms of your hands. Pour off the cloudy liquid through a strainer and then repeat the process two or three more times, until the rinse liquid remains clear.

In a medium-sized saucepan, combine the rinsed and drained quinoa with rice milk. Bring to a slow simmer, then cover and cook for about 15 minutes until the quinoa is tender.

Stir in the remaining ingredients, then transfer about 1-1/2 cups to a blender; purée.

Return puréed mixture to the pan and stir to mix. Serve warm or chilled.

Quinoa Porridge

1/2 cup quinoa
1/4 teaspoon ground cinnamon
1 1/2 cups almond milk
1/2 cup water
2 tablespoons brown sugar
1 teaspoon vanilla extract (optional)
1 pinch salt

Heat a saucepan over medium heat and measure in the quinoa. Season with cinnamon and cook until toasted, stirring frequently, about 3 minutes. Pour in the almond milk, water and vanilla and stir in the brown sugar and salt. Bring to a boil, then cook over low heat until the porridge is thick and grains are tender, about 25 minutes. Add more water if needed if the liquid has dried up before it finishes cooking. Stir occasionally, especially at the end, to prevent burning.

Fruit & Quinoa Breakfast

½ cup low fat almond milk
½ cup water
½ cup quinoa, rinsed
1 cup fresh berries
1 teaspoon ground cinnamon
1/2 cup chopped pecans or almonds, toasted
4 teaspoons agave nectar or stevia sweetener

Combine milk, water and quinoa in a medium saucepan. Bring to a boil over high heat. Reduce heat to medium-low; cover and simmer 15 minutes or until most of the liquid is absorbed. Turn off heat; let stand covered 5 minutes. Stir in berries and cinnamon. Serve, topped with pecans and a drizzle of agave or stevia sweetener

Quinoa-Millet Hot Cereal

1/2 cup quinoa, rinsed and drained
1/4 cup millet, rinsed and drained
2-1/2 cups water
Chopped nuts
Currants, raisins or cranberries
Dried apricots, diced

Bring water and a pinch of salt to a boil in small sauce pan. Add quinoa and millet, stir, cover, reduce heat, and simmer for about 30 minutes. Add a little hot water if it cooks too quickly. The cereal should be neither too watery nor dry (more like porridge).

Serve in a bowl with chopped nuts, dried fruit such as raisins, currants and apricots, along with one to two tablespoons of maple syrup or agave nectar

Breakfast Quinoa Balls

2/3 c. quinoa
1 1/3 c. water
1 1/2 c. whole almonds
1 1/2 T. agave nectar
1/2 tsp. table salt
1 tsp. cinnamon
2 T. brown sugar
1 1/2 tsp. vanilla extract

Preheat the oven to 375 degrees Fahrenheit.

Combine the quinoa and water in a small pot. Heat, covered, over medium heat until it starts to boil. Remove the cover and lower to a simmer. Cook, stirring occasionally, until the quinoa has absorbed all the water. Spread quinoa out on a mat or pan to cool.

Quinoa with Clementine's, Sour Cherries and Pecans

1 cup leftover cooked quinoa
1 cup of almond or rice milk
1 tbsp dried cherries
1 tbsp pecans
2 clementines, broken into segments
A pinch of cinnamon
Agave Nectar to taste

Soak the quinoa and milk together overnight.

When ready to eat, heat the quinoa and milk either in the microwave or in a pan on the hob until hot.

Crumble the pecans roughly into chunks and add to the hot grains and milk. Next add the dried cherries and clementines and a good pinch of cinnamon.

Add agave to taste and eat

Coconut Quinoa Breakfast Cereal

1 cup of quinoa
2 cups of water
½ cup of rice milk
1 tablespoon of maple syrup
Salt
Pineapple bits,
Toasted shredded coconut
½ teaspoon of cinnamon
½ cup of chopped apples, pears, and/or raisins

Rinse and drain 1 cup of quinoa. Over high heat, place the quinoa in the saucepan Add water and salt and boil them Reduce heat to simmer for 5 minutes Add the ½ cup of fruits and continue to simmer until all water is absorbed Serve with rice milk and drizzle maple syrup Add pineapple bits and coconut shreds and cinnamon

Hot Pan Quinoa Breakfast Cereal

1 1/4 cups water
1 cup quinoa
1/4 tsp. ground cinnamon
handful of raisins
1/4 cup sliced almonds

Rinse quinoa in a strainer or cheese cloth. Bring water to a boil in your Hot Pan and add the quinoa. Reduce heat and simmer for 5 minutes. Add the cinnamon and raisins, put the lid on, and place your Hot Pan in its Serving Bowl. Let quinoa stand for 10 minutes (a little more or less won't hurt). Add almonds. Serve with soy milk, and sweeten to taste with sugar.

Quinoa/Almond Hot Cereal

1/3 cup quinoa flakes
3/4 cup water (it called for one cup but I used less)
pinch of sea salt

Cook as it says on box, then stir in the following:

1 tablespoon almond butter
1 tablespoon coconut oil
1/4 cup almond milk
dash of stevia and cinnamon

Quinoa Pancakes

2 cups Organic Quinoa flour
4 tsp baking powder
1/2 tsp sea salt
2 cups + 1 Tb water
2 Tb vegetable oil

Mix dry ingredients in a bowl. Add liquids and whisk to mix. Spoon on heated griddle. Use generous amount of Ghee on the griddle and turn when edges dry. These freeze ok.

Top with your favorite syrup or use just stevia and more ghee as topping.

Quinoa Breakfast

1/2 cup water
1/4 cup quinoa
1/4 cup steel cut oats
1/4 cup crushed pineapple or pineapple juice
1 TB blackstrap molasses
currants or raisins to taste

Rinse the grains.

Boil then simmer the quinoa in water and molasses for ten minutes

Add the oats and fruit and simmer for another 15

variations: try adding vanilla, cinnamon, nut., etc.

Quinoa Pancakes

2 cups organic quinoa flour
4 tsp baking powder
1/2 tsp sea salt
2 cups & 1 tbs water
2 tbs vegetable oil

Directions

Mix dry ingredients in bowl; add liquids; wisk to mix. Preheat pancake griddle. Spoon batter onto hot griddle making pancakes 4-5" across. Turn when edges seem dry (they won't brown much because they don't contain sugar). Keep warm while cooking remaining cakes. Batter may thicken as it stands, if so, stir in 1-2 tbs water as needed. Makes 12 pancakes.

Breakfast Quinoa Cereal

1/2 cup almond or rice milk
2/3 cup water
1/2 cup quinoa
tiny pinch of kosher salt

Optional add-ins all to taste:

dried fruits: raisins, cranberries, chopped apricots, cherries, figs

nuts: chopped and toasted almonds, walnuts, pecans, pine nuts)

fresh fruits of all kinds: stir in right before eating

dried, unsweetened coconut

drizzles: maple syrup, agave nectar

spices: cinnamon, clove, or nutmeg

brown sugar

Rinse quinoa in cold water and drain thoroughly. Place the quinoa, water, milk, and small pinch of salt into a 1.5 – 2 qt. saucepan with a cover. Bring to a rolling boil, then lower the heat to med-low. Simmer for 15 minutes with the saucepan covered, then remove from heat and allow it to stand for 5 additional minutes (or until most, but not all of the liquid is absorbed and most of the quinoa is translucent in the center) with the cover still on.

Stir in add-ins of your choice to taste and serve immediately.

Breakfast Quinoa with Cherries, Walnuts

1 1/3 cups quinoa
2 2/3 cups water
1 small golden delicious apple, unpeeled, cored and cut into chunks
¼ cup dried cherries
½ cup walnuts pieces
½ teaspoon ground cinnamon
2 tablespoons agave nectar, plus more for serving
½ cup almond or rice milk

Put the quinoa in a fine mesh strainer and rinse under the tap.

Put the rinsed quinoa in a saucepan with the water. Bring to a boil, and then reduce heat to simmer, cover and cook for 5 minutes. Add the apples and cherries and continue to cook, covered over a low heat, until the water is absorbed, about 10 minutes more.

In the meantime, toast the walnut in a dry skillet over a medium-high heat, stirring frequently, until they are fragrant, about 2 minutes. Allow them to cool, and then coarsely chop them.

When the quinoa is cooked, stir in the cinnamon, agave and milk of your choice, and cook for 1 more minute, so the milk is heated through.

Place into serving bowls and top with walnuts. Serve with additional agave and milk of choice to taste. Makes 4 servings.

Cinnamon Apple Quinoa Breakfast Cereal

1 C uncooked quinoa
2 C water
1/2 t salt
2 C apples
1 t cinnamon

Rinse quinoa under cold water until the run-off is clear. Bring the water to a boil with the salt. Add quinoa. Reduce heat and allow to simmer for 15 minutes. Remove from heat. Fluff the quinoa and let sit covered for another 10 minutes. Peel and chop apples. microwave for 2 minutes. Add apples and cinnamon to the quinoa. Add whatever other flavors you typically like in your oatmeal.

Quinoa Porridge

1/2 cup uncooked quinoa (rinse!!)
1/2 cup water
1 cup almond or soy milk
1/4 tsp cinnamon
1 tbsp chopped pecans
1 tbsp raisins
1 tsp agave nectar

Add quinoa, water, cinnamon and 1/2 cup of the milk in a pot and bring to a boil. Reduce heat, cover and simmer for 10-15 minutes or until most of the water has been absorbed.

Add the remaining 1/2 cup of milk, pecans and raisins and allow to simmer for about 5 minutes or until it reaches your desired consistency (it will gradually get thicker). Once it reaches the consistency you like, add the agave and stir to combine.

Quinoa Cereal

1/2 cup quinoa
1/4 teaspoon ground cinnamon
1 pinch nutmeg (less than 1/8 teaspoon)
1 1/2 cups almond or soy milk
1/2 cup water
2 tablespoons brown sugar
1 teaspoon vanilla extract
1 pinch salt

Heat a saucepan over medium heat. Add quinoa, cinnamon, and nutmeg. Stir frequently for 3 minutes until toasted.

Add milk, water, and vanilla. Then stir in the brown sugar and salt. Bring to a boil. Simmer over very low heat until it is thick and grains are tender, about 30 minutes. Add more water if needed if the liquid has dried up before it finishes cooking. Stir occasionally, especially at the end, to prevent burning.

Top with raisins or dried cranberries.

Quinoa Pancakes

2 cups quinoa flour
2 Tbs baking powder
1/4 tsp baking soda
1/8 cup light-flavored oil, such as sunflower
1/2 cup raw cashews
2 cups warm water
1 tsp vanilla extract
1 tsp lemon juice or 1/4 tsp (1g) ascorbic acid crystals dissolved in 2 Tbsp (30mL) warm water
1 tsp maple syrup

In a mixing bowl, whisk together quinoa flour, baking powder, and baking soda. In blender, grind nuts to a fine powder, pausing to scrape under the blades 2–3 times. Add to blender: water, vanilla extract, lemon juice, and maple syrup and blend 3–4 minutes. Pour liquids over dry ingredients and whisk a few times, eliminating lumps. If batter is too thick, add water as necessary.

Pour a scant 1/4 cup (60mL) of batter onto hot non-stick griddle (heated until water dances on it) for each pancake. Serve with fruit sauce or applesauce.

Variations: Add 1–2 Tbsp (10–20g) flaxseed into the blender with the cashews

Quinoa POM Wonderful Blueberry Muffins

2 Cups Whole Wheat Flour
1/2 Cup Rolled Oats
1 teaspoon Ground Cinnamon
2 teaspoon Baking Powder
1 teaspoon Baking Soda
1/4 teaspoon Fine grain sea salt
1 Tablespoon Flaxseeds
1.5 Cups Fresh or Frozen Blueberries
1/2 Cup Chopped Walnuts
2 Cups Cooked Quinoa
1/2 unsweetened apple sauce
1/2 Cup Splenda Granulated (or use 1/2 cup Amber Agave Syrup or 1/2 cup white sugar)
1/4 Cup Dark Brown Sugar, Packed
1/2 Cup Pom Wonderful Juice
Sugar (optional)

Preheat your oven to 375 degrees and lightly grease 12 muffin tins.

In a large bowl, whisk together flour, oats, cinnamon, baking powder and soda, and salt. Grind the flaxseeds to a fine powder using a coffee or spice grinder, and mix them in as well. Add in the blueberries and walnuts, and toss them to coat.

Separately, combine the cooked quinoa, apple sauce, splenda/sugar/agave, brown sugar, and POM Wonderful juice. Once the mixture is well-mixed, pour these wet ingredients into the bowl of dry, and use a wide spatula to combine. Stir only enough to bring the batter together, leaving any small lumps that form in favor of mixing it as little as possible. Distribute the mixture evenly between your prepared tins, and sprinkle with about 1/2 teaspoon sugar per muffin, if desired.

Bake for 18 - 22 minutes, until a toothpick inserted into the center of a muffin comes out clean. Let cool for 10 minutes in the pan before moving them to a wire rack to finish cooling.

Quinoa Muffins Recipe with Pecans and Dark Chocolate Chips

Preheat the oven to 350 degrees F. Line twelve muffin cups with parchment liners.

In a bowl whisk together the dry ingredients:
1 cup Ancient Harvest Quinoa Flakes
1/2 cup sorghum flour
1/2 buckwheat flour
1/4 cup millet flour
1/4 cup potato or tapioca starch
1 teaspoon baking powder
1 teaspoon baking soda
1/2 teaspoon sea salt
1 1/4 teaspoons xanthan gum
1-2 teaspoons cinnamon, to taste

In a mixing bowl, beat together until smooth:
1/4 cup plus 1 tablespoon light olive oil
3/4 cup organic light brown sugar
1 tablespoon bourbon vanilla extract
1/2 to 3/4 cup rice milk, as needed (start with 1/2 cup)
1/4 teaspoon light tasting vinegar
1 tablespoon Ener-G Egg Replacer whisked with 1/4 cup warm water

Add the dry ingredients to the wet mixture and beat to combine. Add a little more rice milk, as needed (I ended up using 3/4 cup) to make a thick but smooth muffin batter.

Add in by hand:
1/2 cup chopped pecans (may omit for nut-free)
2/3 cup dark chocolate chips

Stir the batter to distribute the pecans and chocolate. Drop the batter by spoonfuls into twelve prepared muffin cups. Bake in the center of a preheated oven until golden and firm- about 18 to 20 minutes, depending upon your oven and altitude. Remove muffins from the pan when they are cool enough to handle- cool on a wire rack to prevent soggy bottoms. Serves 12. Wrap in foil and freeze for easy on-the-go breakfast bites.

Chapter 2 - Vegan Quinoa Bread

Tomato Quinoa Bread

1 teaspoon active dry yeast
1 teaspoon sugar
1/3 cup lukewarm water
1 tablespoon extra-virgin olive oil
2 teaspoons fine sea salt
1 cup seasoned vegetable juice
1/2 cup quinoa (un-cooked)
3 3/4 cups (1 pound) bread flour

Mix the yeast, sugar and water together in the bowl of an electric mixer. Let stand for 5 minutes, until foamy then stir in the oil, salt, juice and quinoa.

Fit your stand mixer with the dough hook, set it on medium-low speed and add the flour in a little at a time. Mix until most of the flour is incorporated and the dough comes together in a ball. Continue to mix for 4-5 minutes more, until the dough becomes soft and shiny, but still firm. If the dough is too sticky, add a bit more flour.

Cover the bowl with plastic wrap and refrigerate until the dough has doubled or tripled in size, this should take 8 to 12 hours. The dough may also be left in the refrigerator for up to two days, but you may need to punch it down a few times as it doubles.

Take the dough out of the refrigerator and punch it down. Form the dough into a ball, return to the bowl and cover with plastic wrap. Allow the dough to double once again; this should take about an hour.

Punch the dough down one more time, then form it into a tight rectangle. Place the dough into a rectangular bread pan, cover with a cloth and let rise until double in size.

Oven preheated to 450, slash the top of the loaf with a very sharp knife so that it can expand properly and place on the middle rack of the oven. Bake for 45 minutes, until the crust is golden brown and it sounds hollow when tapped. Turn the loaf out on a rack to cool and wait at least 1 hour before slicing.

Vegan Yeast-Free Quinoa Bread

2 cups gluten-free high-fiber flour blend
2 cups gluten-free high-protein flour blend
¼ cup golden flax meal
3/4 teaspoon salt
2 tablespoons baking powder
1 1/4 teaspoons baking soda
2 teaspoons xanthan gum
½ cup cooked whole-grain quinoa or millet, cooked
1 1/2 cups sparkling cider, apple cider or apple juice concentrate
½ cup unsweetened applesauce
¼ cup oil of choice
1 tablespoon agave nectar
1 tablespoon apple cider vinegar
Rice Milk of choice, for topping
2 tablespoons quinoa flakes, for topping
Oil spray, for topping
Rice flour or cornmeal for dusting

Preheat oven to 400 degrees. Lightly grease a 9x4-inch bread pan and sprinkle with cornmeal or rice flour. Blend together the flour blends, flax meal, salt, baking powder, baking soda and xanthan gum in a mixing bowl until well combined. Fold in cooked quinoa.

In a separate bowl, whisk together the cider, applesauce, oil, agave and vinegar. Pour the wet ingredients into the dry and mix together on medium speed using the beater/paddle attachment until just combined. Do not over mix.

Pour dough into prepared bread pan. Brush the top with rice milk of choice, sprinkle with quinoa flakes and lightly spray with oil. Loosely cover bread pan with parchment paper or oiled foil and bake in preheated oven for 30 minutes. Remove the paper and bake another 15 to 20 minutes or until the top is brown and internal temperature reaches 200 degrees. Cool in the pan for 5 minutes. Then lift the loaf out onto a wire rack to cool.

Sprouted Quinoa Superfood Bread

5 cup sprouted quinoa flour
¼ cup maca
2 tablespoon mesquite
2 teaspoon real salt
½ cup chia seeds
1½ cup water
1 cup olive oil
10 dates
2 zucchini, roughly chopped

To make the quinoa flour, soak 3-4 cups of dry quinoa for about 4 hours. Drain water and let sit for a day or so (Rinse once or twice during this time). You'll soon see the little tails, and it will be ready to go. Spread the sprouts on dehydrator sheets and dry at a low heat for 4-5 hours. When dry to touch, grind in batches in a blender or coffee grinder. In a large mixing bowl, combine the dry ingredients and mix together: quinoa flour, maca, mesquite, salt.

In a separate bowl, combine the chia seeds with the 1 1/2 cups of water and set aside.

In a blender, combine the olive oil, dates and zucchini. Add this to the chia goop and mix well. Then combine the dry and wet ingredients in the large bowl and mix well with a spoon (and/or your hands) until well combined.

Divide the dough into four equal parts. Using an offset spatula spread the mix on dehydrator sheets to an even thickness. Or, place a second sheet on top of the dough and roll out with a rolling pin. Trim the edges so you have a big square shape.

Dehydrate for several hours before flipping, scoring (I do 9 equal squares) and returning to dehydrate without the teflex sheets until the bread is to your preferred texture.

Yummy Quinoa Bread

1/4 tsp. Active Dry Yeast
1 tsp. Cinnamon or Allspice
3/4 C. Tapioca Flour
3/4 can or more Apple Juice Concentrate , thawed
1 T. Lecithin or Oil
3/4 tsp Salt
1 C. Water, luke warm
2 1/2 C Quinoa Flour
1/2 C Raisins
2 T Oil

For Breadmachine:

Whisk all dry ingredients together first before starting to add in. Add in order in a Breadman bread machine or reverse order as your bread machine directions dictate. Don't add the raisins in until the dough is thoroughly mixed. Push the gluten free setting for a 1.5 lb. loaf. Assist the machine in the mixing process by mixing with a spatula until it looks like a thicker quick bread consistency.

Directions by Mixer/Oven:

Whisk all dry ingredients together first. Then in a mixer add liquid ingredients. Add the dry ingredients to the wets. Mix for 10 minutes, let rest for 5 minutes,mix for 15 minutes, let rise in a greased bread pan for 60 minutes in a warm place with plastic wrap over it. After it rises, place in a oven that was preheated to 350* to 375* and bake for 50

Whole Wheat Quinoa Bread

1 1/4 cups water
1 Tsp light olive oil with a dash of toasted sesame oil
2 Tsp. agave nectar
1/2 tsp salt
1 3/4 cups bread flour
1 3/4 cups whole wheat flour
1/3 cup uncooked quinoa
1 3/4 tsp. active dry yeast

TO MAKE BY MACHINE: 1. Place the ingredients in the order listed in your bread machine. Set it for Whole Wheat with a dark crust if you have that option.

TO MAKE BY HAND: 1. Dissolve the yeast in 1/4 cup of lukewarm water and let stand for 10 minutes. 2. Combine the remaining 1 cup of water, the oil, agave, and dissolved yeast in a small bowl. Combine the salt, bread flour, whole wheat flour, and quinoa in a large bowl. Pour the liquid into the dry ingredients and mix until you have a smooth ball. Knead for 10 minutes on a lightly floured board. Place the dough in a lightly oiled mixing bowl, cover with a clean kitchen towel, and let rise until double in volume, about 1 1/2 hours. 3. Punch the dough down, form into a loaf shape, and place in an oiled 9 x 5 x 3-inch loaf pan. Cover with the towel and let it rise again until double its original size, about 1 hour. 4. Bake at 350 F (180 C) for 45 minutes to 1 hour or until an instant-read thermometer registers 190 F (88 C). Set on a rack to cool. Slice and enjoy

Gluten Free Quinoa Crackers

100g (3.5 oz) quinoa grain (seeds) or flour
50g (2oz) potato flour (farina)
¼ tsp salt
80ml (3fl oz) water

If you are using quinoa grain (seeds), soak in warm water for a minute to remove the soapy bitter taste it can have. Heat a dry skillet or frying pan on the hob. Rinse quinoa in a sieve, add to hot pan to dry off and toast slightly (2 minutes).

Remove pan from heat and carefully pour grain into a liquidizer or coffee grinder and zap to turn into flour.

Decant into a mixing bowl, add the potato flour, salt and the water. Mix into a dough. Form the dough into 6 pieces about the size of a golf ball. Reheat the skillet/pan. Roll the dough out between cling film (saran wrap) as thinly as you can handle and cook in the pan for about 1½ minutes on each side. Repeat with remaining dough.

Can be used immediately as unleavened bread or if you allow to cool turns into a reasonable cracker

Quinoa Whole Wheat Bread Recipe

1 cup, whole uncooked quinoa
2 cups warm water
1 tbsp raw sugar
1 tbsp active dry yeast
2 cups whole wheat flour
1½ cups all purpose flour
2 tbsp vital wheat gluten flour
1 tsp salt

Thoroughly rinse quinoa in a sieve under a running tap.

In a small bowl combine half the water, the yeast and the sugar. Leave for 10 minutes until frothy on top.

In a large bowl combine flours, quinoa and salt. Make a well in the centre of the flours and pour in water/yeast.

Mix well with your hand until water is soaked up. Gradually add remaining water as needed, until a soft, moist dough is formed.

Place dough on a floured surface and knead for 5 minutes.

Place dough in a large, oiled bowl and cover with a dish towel. Leave to prove in a warm, draught-free place for about 1½ hours, until doubled in size.

Knock air out of dough by kneading for another minute or so. Now make it in to the desired shape. Score across top of loaves with a knife if desired. Place on oiled baking tray or tin and leave to prove for another 1½ hours.

Preheat oven to 400F (200c). Bake loaves for around 30 minutes, until brown and sound hollow when tapped.

Healthy Flat Bread

1 cup cooked buckwheat
1 cup cooked quinoa
1/4 tsp sea salt
3 tbsp Extra Virgin Olive Oil
other spices

Preheat oven to 350

Cook the grains according to package

Add all ingredients to the food processor and blend

Roll out mixture onto a backing sheet and bake for 30-40 minutes. You can do it longer if you would like the flat breads more crispy and dry.

Quinoa Wheat Bread (No Bread Machine)

1 cup whole quinoa (uncooked and rinsed)
2 cups warm water (just nuke it, 50 seconds per cup)
1 heaping tablespoon brown sugar (give or take, as desired)
.25 oz of active dry yeast (or 1 packet)
1 teaspoon salt (I used sea salt)
2 cups whole wheat flour
1.5 cups all-purpose bread flour (all-purpose)
1-2 tablespoons vital wheat gluten (optional)
1/2 cup of rye flakes (optional, exchangeable for oats, etc..)
2 tablespoons sesame oil

In a small bowl combine 1 cup warm water with yeast and sugar, stir. Rinse quinoa (just fill a bowl with water and strained it twice).

In a large bowl mix salt, whole wheat and bread (all-purpose) flours, and quinoa. Add yeast, sugar, and water to the large bowl as well.

Mix with your hands, Add the second cup of warm water ONLY as needed. Mix until moist dough has formed.

Knead on a floured surface for about 5 minutes

Put the dough (it will still be sticky) into a different large bowl that has been coated with the oil. Cover with a dish towel, do not use cling wrap. Let sit in a warm spot for 2 hours.

When the dough is done rising, knead for a minute or two. It will noticeably shrink..

Lightly flour the bottom of the pan you'll be baking your bread in. Make your dough into the shape you want, you can make a single loaf, multiple loaves, or rolls.

Add the rye flakes or oats on top.

Chapter 3 - Vegan Salad Recipes

Cranberry Walnut Quinoa Salad

1 cup quinoa
1 cup dried cranberries
1 cup frozen green beans, defrosted
1/4 cup walnuts, chopped
1/4 cup green onions, sliced
1/4 cup balsamic vinegar
1 1/2 tablespoons olive oil
4 cloves garlic, minced
1/2 teaspoon salt
1/4 teaspoon pepper

Combine quinoa with 2 cups water in a medium saucepan and bring to a boil over high heat. Reduce heat to a simmer, cover, and continue cooking until all water is absorbed.

In a medium bowl, combine cooked quinoa, dried cranberries, green beans, walnuts, and green onions until well mixed. In a small bowl, whisk the balsamic vinegar, olive oil, and garlic until well blended. Pour over the quinoa mixture. Toss until well blended. Season with salt and pepper, to taste. Chill in the refrigerator for at least 30 minutes before serving

Easy Vegan Quinoa Salad

1 cup Quinoa
1 ½ Cup Cold Water
½ tsp. Salt
1-2 Small Carrots peeled and sliced thin
1 Cup Snow Peas, Shell Peas, Celery or Green Beans
½ Green or Red Pepper, sliced thin
1 Medium Ripe Tomato
1 Medium Cucumber, peeled and diced
¼ cup Chopped fresh Parsley Cilantro, or Basil
½ cup Chopped walnuts, toasted sunflower seeds or toasted cashews
Options: Chopped scallions, dried unsweetened cranberries, raisins or apricots, Greek olives, minced Jalapeno pepper, fresh mint

Dressing:

2 Tbsp. freshly squeezed lemon juice
¼ cup Olive Oil
½ tsp. Salt
Fresh ground pepper
Options: Pinch of cayenne garlic powder or fresh minced garlic minced fresh or dried ginger.

Quinoa Salad Directions

Soak quinoa 15 minutes in cold water Rinse thoroughly, drain through a large fine mesh strainer Place in 2 qt pot with the water, salt and oil Bring to a boil

Turn the heat down to very low, cover and cook for 15 minutes Remove from heat and allow to sit five minutes with lid on Fluff gently with a fork and set aside to cook. Setting the pan in a sink full

Of cold water cools quickly Steam the carrots and green veg for 5 min, rinse in cold water Chop the tomatoes, herb and cucumber Blend dressing ingredients with a whisk or shake in a jar Gently combine veggies, walnuts, quinoa and dressing in a large bowl Cover and chill

Greek Quinoa Salad

3-4 cups water or vegetable broth
1 1/2 cups quinoa, uncooked
1/4 cup apple cider vinegar (you may use any flavor you prefer)
2 cloves garlic, minced
juice from one lemon
3 tbsp olive oil
1/2 cup kalamata olives, sliced if desired
1/3 cup fresh parsley, chopped
1/3 cup fresh cilantro, chopped
1 red onion, diced
1 cup cherry tomatoes, sliced in half
1/2 cup chopped artichoke hearts (optional)
salt and pepper to taste

Preparation:

In a medium-large saucepan, cook the quinoa in vegetable broth for 15-20 minutes, until tender, stirring occasionally. Allow to cool.

In a small bowl, whisk together the vinegar, lemon juice, garlic, and olive oil.

Gently toss the quinoa together with the remaining ingredients. Pour the olive oil mixture over the quinoa.

Add more salt and pepper to taste.

You may also add any additional vegetables that you like, such as lightly steamed broccoli, snap peas or diced bell pepper.

Mediterranean Quinoa Salad

1 cup quinoa, rinsed
2 cups water
2 cloves garlic, crushed
1/2 cup chopped scallions
1 cup cherry tomatoes, halved
1 cup cucumber, chopped
1/2 cup radish, chopped
2 tablespoons fresh mint, chopped
2 tablespoons coriander / cilantro, chopped
1 cup finely chopped parsley
1 small bunch watercress, chopped
1/4 cup freshly squeezed lemon juice
1/4 cup extra virgin olive oil
1/2 cup black olives, pitted
salt and pepper, freshly ground to taste

Bring quinoa and water to boil, cover and simmer on a low heat for 20 mins. Let quinoa cool to room temperature, then transfer to a serving bowl.

Mix the garlic and scallions thoroughly with the quinoa and add the remaining chopped herbs and vegetables. Stir in the lemon juice and extra virgin olive oil. Finally, mix in the olives and season with freshly ground salt and pepper.

Set aside for at least 30 mins before serving to allow the flavors to develop and blend.

Egg Plant Avocado Quinoa Salad

1 small eggplant, chopped
1/2 cup quinoa
1 cup chopped flat leaf parsley
1 bunch scallions, chopped
1 pint grape tomatoes, sliced in half
5 tablespoons olive oil
juice of 1/2 lemon
salt
sliced avocado and hummus for serving (optional)

Preheat oven to 400. Toss the eggplant with 1 tablespoon of the olive oil and sprinkle with salt. Roast until tender, about 20 minutes (roasting time may vary depending on how coarsely you chop the eggplant).

Meanwhile, cook quinoa according to package directions. Toss quinoa, eggplant, tomatoes, parsley and scallions together in a large bowl. Meanwhile, whisk together the remaining 4 tablespoons olive oil and the juice of 1/2 a lemon.

Season with salt and pepper and add more lemon juice if necessary. Pour the dressing over the quinoa and toss to coat. Refrigerate the salad for about an hour to allow the flavors to blend. If using, top with sliced avocado and a couple of dollops of hummus.

Quinoa Red Pepper Cherry Salad

1/4 cup quinoa
1/4 chopped red pepper
1/4 cup shelled edamame
1/8 diced onion
1/8 cup dried tart cherries

White Wine Vinaigrette Dressing
2 tbsp olive oil
2 tbsp white wine vinegar
1 tsp Dijon mustard
Pinch sugar
Salt and pepper to taste
2 tbsp sunflower seeds, shelled

Preparation:

Cook quinoa, cool and toss with red pepper, edamame, onion, and dried tart cherries.

For white wine vinaigrette dressing, whisk together olive oil, white wine vinegar, Dijon mustard, and sugar. Add salt and pepper. Mix 2 tbsp dressing (or more to taste) into salad and sprinkle with 2 tbsp shelled sunflower seeds.

Quinoa and Grilled-Pepper Salad

1 1/4 cups quinoa
3 yellow and/or orange bell peppers, quartered
2 teaspoons extra-virgin olive oil
1 teaspoon fresh lime juice
1 teaspoon soy sauce
1/2 teaspoon ground cumin
1/4 cup chopped fresh cilantro
3 scallions, chopped

Prepare grill for cooking.

Wash quinoa in at least 5 changes of water, rubbing grains and letting them settle before pouring off water, until water runs clear. Drain in a large sieve. Add quinoa to a saucepan of boiling salted water and cook 10 minutes. Drain in sieve and rinse under cold water.

Set sieve over a saucepan with 1 1/2 inches boiling water (sieve should not touch water) and steam quinoa, covered with a kitchen towel and lid, until fluffy and dry, about 10 minutes. (Check water level in pan occasionally, adding water if necessary.) Spread quinoa on a baking sheet to cool.

While quinoa is cooking, grill bell peppers on a well-oiled rack set 5 to 6 inches over glowing coals until slightly softened, about 4 minutes on each side. Cut bell peppers crosswise into thin strips.

Whisk together oil, lime juice, soy sauce, and cumin in a large bowl and stir in quinoa, bell peppers, cilantro, scallions, and salt and pepper to taste.

Curried Quinoa Salad with Mango

1 cup quinoa (about 6 ounces)
1/4 cup canola oil
2 tablespoons white wine vinegar
1 tablespoon mango chutney, chopped if chunky
1 1/2 teaspoons curry powder
1/4 teaspoon dry mustard
1 cup chopped peeled mango plus mango spears for garnish
1 cup chopped unpeeled English hothouse cucumber
5 tablespoons chopped green onions, divided
2 cups (packed) baby spinach

Preparation:

Cook quinoa in medium pot of boiling salted water over medium heat until tender but still firm to bite, stirring occasionally, about 12 minutes. Drain well; cool. Transfer to medium bowl.

Meanwhile, whisk oil and next 4 ingredients in small bowl to blend. Season dressing to taste with salt and pepper.

Add chopped mango, cucumber, 4 tablespoons green onions, and 1/4 cup dressing to quinoa; toss to coat. Divide spinach between 2 plates. Spoon quinoa salad over spinach. Garnish with mango spears and 1 tablespoon green onions. Drizzle with remaining dressing; serve.

To chop a mango:

Cut mango in half lengthwise, slicing around the pit. Cut a half-inch grid into flesh of each half. Using your thumbs, push up skin side so cubes stick out. Slice off cubes at base.

Quinoa Salad with Asparagus and Fresh Basil

2 cup water
1 Tablespoon Soy Sauce
1 1/2 cups Quinoa washed and drained
2 Tablespoons Extra Virgin Olive Oil
1 pound asparagus, steamed until tender and crisp, cut into 1/2 inch pieces
3 Tablespoons lemon juice, freshly squeezed
1/2 cup roasted red peppers, diced
1/2 cup fresh basil, chopped
1/4 cup fresh chives, minced or sliced green onions

Garnishes
1 small head of radicchio or leaf lettuce
1 pint organic cherry tomatoes

Directions

Bring water to a boil in a quart sauce pan. Add soy sauce and quinoa. Cover and return to a boil. Reduce the heat and simmer for about 15 minutes, until the quinoa is tender but still crunchy.

Place quinoa in a mixing bowl and toss with the olive oil. When the quinoa has cooled to room temperature, mix in the asparagus, lemon juice, red peppers, basil and chives. Add more tamari to taste, if desired. Serve on a bed of radicchio leaves surrounded by cherry tomatoes.

Quinoa Olive Medley

2 cups Quinoa washed and drained
2 1/2 cups water, for cooking quinoa
2/3 cup pitted black olives, cut in half
2/3 cup pitted green olives, cut in half
1/4 cup pine nuts, lightly pan toasted
1 cup green onions, finely chopped
1/4 cup fresh parsley, finely chopped
1/3 cup red bell pepper, cut into thin strips
2 cloves garlic, finely minced
2 Tablespoons Extra Virgin Olive Oil
2 teaspoons Ume Plum Vinegar, or to taste

Directions

Cook quinoa according to package directions. Toss to cool, then mix in remaining ingredients, adding ume plum vinegar last and seasoning to taste.

Quinoa Tabouli Salad

2 cups Quinoa, washed and drained
3 cups water
14 1/2 ounces Diced Tomatoes, drained
1 medium cucumber, peeled, seeded and diced
1 cup green onions, chopped
1 Tablespoon dried mint leaves or 5 minced fresh mint leaves
2 Tablespoons Extra Virgin Olive Oil
1 Tablespoon Ume Plum Vinegar, or to taste
2 cloves garlic, pressed
3/4 cup fresh parsley, finely chopped

Cook quinoa according to package directions. Remove and toss to cool. Combine quinoa, parsley, tomatoes, cucumber, garlic, green onions, and mint. Mix well. Combine olive oil, ume plum vinegar and garlic. Mix into the salad.

Quinoa with Mint and Pine Nuts

2/3 cup Quinoa, washed and drained
1 1/4 cups water
2 teaspoons Soy Sauce
1/3 cup pine nuts, lightly pan toasted
3 1/2 Tablespoons scallions, finely chopped
2 1/2 Tablespoons fresh mint leaves, chopped
2/3 cup cauliflower, small florets, blanched 2 minutes

Place the quinoa and water in a sauce pan, cover and bring to a boil. Reduce flame to medium-low and simmer for 20 minutes. Remove, place in a bowl and allow to cool for a few minutes. Sprinkle the soy sauce, pine nuts, scallions, cauliflower and mint. Mix and serve.

Quinoa Navy Bean Salad

1 1/2 cups Organic Quinoa, washed and drained
1 1/2 cups organic sweet corn, fresh or frozen
1/2 cup green peas, fresh or frozen
2 1/4 cups water
1/2 cup green bell pepper, diced
1/2 cup roasted red peppers, chopped
1/2 cup red onion, minced
1 cup fresh basil, finely chopped
15 ounces Organic Navy Beans, drained or cooked Eden Organic Dry Navy Beans
2 cloves garlic, minced
1 1/2 Tablespoons Extra Virgin Olive Oil
1/4 cup lemon juice, freshly squeezed
1 Tablespoon Ume Plum Vinegar, or to taste
Several Lettuce Leaves

Directions

Place quinoa, water, corn and peas in a sauce pan. Cover, bring to a boil, reduce flame to low and simmer for 12 to 15 minutes.

Remove and place in a large mixing bowl. Toss with a spoon or fork to fluff and cool the quinoa. Add the red onion, basil, roasted pepper and navy beans. Blend the lemon juice, garlic, olive oil and ume plum vinegar in a blender.

Pour over the quinoa and vegetables. Mix in thoroughly and serve on a bed of lettuce.

Sweet Plum Salad

1 1/4 cup quinoa
2 1/2 cup water
2 fresh California plums, pitted and diced
1/2 cup chopped, toasted walnuts
1/4 cup each: chopped red and yellow bell pepper
1/4 cup sliced green onions
3 tablespoon each: flax oil and extra virgin olive oil
1/4 cup white wine vinegar
1 1/2 tablespoon agave nectar
1/4 teaspoon salt

Directions

Rinse quinoa and drain well. Add to boiling water; reduce heat and simmer, covered, for 12 minutes.

Remove from heat and let stand for 5 minutes. Fluff with a fork and let chill for about 30 minutes.

Stir together quinoa, plums, walnuts, peppers and onions in a medium bowl.

Whisk together remaining ingredients in a small bowl and pour over salad; toss well to coat all ingredients with dressing.

Cover and chill for 1 hour.

Quinoa Vegetable Salad

1 1/2 cups Quinoa, washed and drained
1 1/2 cups water
1/2 cup green bell pepper, diced
1/2 cup roasted red peppers, packed in oil or water, chopped
1/2 cup red onion, minced
1 1/2 cups organic sweet corn, fresh or frozen
1/2 cup green peas, fresh or frozen
1 cup fresh basil, finely chopped
2 cloves garlic, minced
1 1/2 Tablespoons Extra Virgin Olive Oil
1/4 cup lemon juice, freshly squeezed
15 ounces   Navy Beans, drained or Garbanzo Beans
1 Tablespoon Ume Plum Vinegar, or to taste
Several Lettuce Leaves

Directions

Place quinoa, water, corn and peas in a sauce pan. Cover, reduce flame to low and simmer for 12 to 15 minutes. Remove and place in a large mixing bowl. Toss with a spoon or fork to fluff and cool the quinoa.

Add the red onion, basil, roasted peppers and navy beans. Blend the lemon juice, garlic, olive oil and ume plum vinegar in a blender. Pour over the quinoa and vegetables. Mix in thoroughly and serve on a bed of lettuce.

Quinoa Salsa Salad

2 cups Quinoa, washed and drained
2 1/2 cups cold water
15 ounces Garbanzo Beans, drained
1 medium cucumber, diced
1 medium yellow summer squash, diced, blanched 1 minute
6 ounces pitted olives

Salsa
14 1/2 ounces Diced Tomatoes w/Green Chilies, do not drain
2 cloves garlic, finely minced
1 cup red onion, finely chopped
1/4 cup orange juice
1/2 teaspoon ground cumin
1 pinch ground coriander
1/8 teaspoon freshly ground black pepper
2 Tablespoons Red Wine Vinegar
2 teaspoons Ume Plum Vinegar, or to taste
1/2 cup fresh parsley, finely chopped

Directions

Place the quinoa and water in a medium saucepan, cover and bring to a boil. Reduce the flame and simmer for 20 minutes. Remove from the pan and place in a large mixing bowl. Fluff to cool. When cool add the cucumber, summer squash, olives and garbanzo beans.

To prepare the salsa, mix all the ingredients together. Pour the salsa over the quinoa and vegetables. Toss to mix thoroughly. Serve room temperature or chilled.

Quinoa Salpicon (Spicy Quinoa Salad)

14 1/2 ounces Diced Tomatoes w/Green Chilies, drained, reserve liquid
2 cups water, including drained tomato cooking liquid
1/2 teaspoon Sea Salt
1 clove garlic, minced
1 1/2 cups Quinoa, rinsed and drained
1 small cucumber, seeded and diced, peeled if waxed
1 medium avocado, pit removed, peeled and diced
1/2 cup fresh cilantro, minced fresh parsley
1/3 cup red onion, minced
1 small jalapeno pepper, seeded and minced, optional
1 Tablespoon Extra Virgin Olive Oil
1/3 cup lime juice, freshly squeezed

Directions

Drain the tomatoes, place the tomato liquid in a measuring cup and add enough cold water to equal 2 cups. Bring the tomato/water mixture, sea salt and garlic to a boil. Stir in the quinoa and return to a boil. Cover and simmer for 15 to 20 minutes until the quinoa is tender. Turn off the flame and let sit, covered, for 5 minutes. Transfer to a large serving bowl and fluff up.

Gently toss in the remaining ingredients, including the diced tomatoes, using enough lime juice to give the salad a pleasant flavor.

Toasted Quinoa Salad

3/4 cup uncooked quinoa
1-1/2 cups water
1 cup diced carrots
1/2 cup chopped red bell pepper
1/4 cup minced fresh parsley
2 sliced green onions
1 to 2 tablespoons fresh squeezed lemon juice
1 to 2 tablespoons fresh squeezed lime juice
1-1/2 tablespoons soy sauce or tamari
2 cloves garlic, minced
1 teaspoon chili sauce (Tabasco)

Directions:

Rinse quinoa and drain. Put quinoa in a pot over medium-high heat and dry toast until a few grains begin to pop.

Add water, bring to a boil, cover and simmer for 15 minutes, or until quinoa has absorbed all the liquid. Remove from heat and let stand for 10 minutes. Fluff with a fork and let cool.

Mix carrots, pepper, parsley and green onions in a large bowl. Add quinoa and toss to combine. In a small bowl, whisk together lemon and lime juices, soy sauce or tamari, garlic and chili sauce.

Pour over salad and combine well. Chill until serving time.

Scarlet Quinoa

1 cup Quinoa, washed and drained
1 1/2 cups water or vegetable stock
1/3 cup diced beets
2 Tablespoons Extra Virgin Olive Oil
1 Tablespoon Ume Plum Vinegar, or to taste
1 Tablespoon freshly squeezed lemon juice
1/2 teaspoon freshly grated lemon zest (rind)
6 whole red radishes, sliced into half-moons
2 Tablespoons minced red onion
1/4 cup chopped scallions or chives
2 ounces Dried Cranberries

Cook quinoa together with the beets in water according to package directions. When done, cool, toss with all remaining ingredients and serve.

Minted Quinoa with Crunchy Pine Nuts

1 cup Quinoa, washed and drained1 1/4 cup water
1 Tablespoon Ume Plum Vinegar, or to taste
1/2 cup pine nuts, lightly pan toasted
1/3 cup scallions, finely chopped
1/4 cup fresh mint leaves, chopped fine
1 cup cauliflower, small florets, blanched 2 minutes
1/4 cup carrots, diced, blanched 1 minute
2 Tablespoons Extra Virgin Olive Oil

Place the quinoa and water in a sauce pan, cover and bring to a boil. Reduce flame to medium-low and simmer for 15 minutes. Remove, place in a bowl and allow to cool for a few minutes. Sprinkle ume plum vinegar, olive oil, pine nuts, scallions, cauliflower, carrots and mint on top. Toss and serve.

Quinoa with Black Soybeans

15 ounces Black Soybeans, 1 can, drained, reserve liquid
1 1/2 teaspoons Soy Sauce
2 cups water, including reserved bean cooking liquid
1/4 cup snow peas, remove stems
1 1/3 cups Quinoa, washed and drained
1/2 cup scallions, keep bulb and green part separate, slice thin
2 cloves garlic, chopped
1/2 cup roasted red peppers, finely chopped
1/4 cup Hot Pepper Sesame Oil
1 teaspoon Brown Rice Vinegar

Combine the soybeans and soy sauce in a small bowl. Cover, and mix occasionally. Place water in a heavy saucepan, and bring to a boil. Blanch the snow peas for 30 seconds. Remove, rinse, drain, and set aside. Place the quinoa, garlic, and white bulb part of the scallions in the boiling water. Cover, bring to a boil, and reduce the flame to medium-low. Simmer for 20 minutes.

While the quinoa is cooking, thinly slice the snow peas, and place them in a mixing bowl. Add the beans, red pepper, and sliced scallion greens. Toss in the quinoa and thoroughly mix in the hot pepper sesame oil and rice vinegar. Serve warm over steamed kale or at room temperature on a bed of watercress, leaf lettuce or radicchio.

Quinoa Tabbouleh

2 cups Quinoa, washed and drained
2 1/2 cups water
14 1/2 ounces Diced Tomatoes, well drained
1 medium cucumber, peeled if waxed, chopped
1 cup fresh parsley, finely minced
1/3 cup fresh mint leaves, finely minced
1/2 cup pitted black olives
1/2 cup red onion, finely minced
1/3 cup lemon juice, freshly squeezed
1 Tablespoon Ume Plum Vinegar
3 Tablespoons Extra Virgin Olive Oil
4 ounces Roasted Pumpkin Seeds, 1 package

Bring the water to a boil in a medium saucepan, add the quinoa, cover, reduce the flame to medium-low and simmer for 15 minutes or until all water has been absorbed. Place the quinoa in a large mixing bowl and fluff with a spoon until room temperature. Add all remaining ingredients and mix thoroughly before transferring to a serving bowl.

Quinoa Blueberry Walnut & Garbanzo Salad

1 cup Quinoa, rinsed well and drained
1 1/2 cups water
1 pinch Sea Salt
4 ounces Dried Wild Blueberries or Dried Cranberries
1 cup green peas, fresh or frozen blanched 2 minutes, rinsed and drained
1/3 cup walnuts, lightly dry pan roasted and coarsely chopped
1 cup Garbanzo Beans, drained and rinsed
1/3 cup red onion, finely chopped
2 Tablespoons fresh chives, finely chopped
1 clove garlic, minced
3 Tablespoons Brown Rice Vinegar
1 Tablespoon Ume Plum Vinegar
2 Tablespoons Extra Virgin Olive Oil
1/4 teaspoon finely ground black pepper, or to taste
2 heads Boston lettuce, washed and drained

Place quinoa, water and sea salt in a medium pot, cover and bring to a boil. Reduce the flame to medium-low and simmer for 15 minutes or until all water is absorbed. While the quinoa is cooking prepare the dressing by mixing together the vinegars, olive oil and pepper in a small bowl and set aside.

When the quinoa is done, place in a mixing bowl, and fluff with a fork to cool. When room temperature, add all remaining ingredients and pour the dressing over. Gently toss to mix. Refrigerate for 30 minutes before serving. Serve over a bed of lettuce leaves.

Crimson Quinoa

1 1/2 cups Quinoa, washed and drained
2 1/4 cups water
1 pinch Sea Salt
1 cup beets, peeled and grated
1/2 cup fresh parsley, packed and finely minced
1/2 cup scallions, chopped
2 1/2 Tablespoons Extra Virgin Olive Oil
1/2 cup lemon juice, freshly squeezed
3 cups baby salad greens, for garnish
1 medium carrot, julienned, for garnish

Place quinoa, water and salt in a saucepan and cook as package directs.

Remove, fluff up the quinoa, stir in the beets until all the grains turn scarlet. Stir in the parsley, scallions, olive oil and lemon juice.

Serve on a bed of salad greens surrounded with carrot sticks. May be served warm, room temperature or chilled. Additional lemon juice and Sea Salt may be added, if desired.

Colorful Quinoa Medley

2 cups Quinoa, washed and drained
2 1/4 cups water
14 1/2 ounces Diced Tomatoes, drained
1 medium cucumber, peeled if waxed, seeded and chopped
1 cup scallions, sliced
3 cloves garlic, minced
3/4 cup fresh parsley, minced
3/4 cup pine nuts, lightly pan toasted
1/2 cup pitted black olives, sliced thin
1/2 cup roasted red peppers, drained and diced

Dressing
2 Tablespoons Extra Virgin Olive Oil
1 1/4 Tablespoon Ume Plum Vinegar, or to taste
2 teaspoons lime juice, freshly squeezed

Bring the water to a boil in a medium saucepan. Add the quinoa, cover and bring to a boil again. Reduce the flame and simmer for 12 minutes. Turn off flame and let sit for 5 minutes. Place quinoa in a large mixing bowl and fluff with a fork to cool. Add the tomatoes, cucumber, scallions, garlic, parsley, pine nuts, olives and red peppers. In a small bowl, mix the dressing ingredients together. Pour the dressing over the salad and toss to mix thoroughly. Serve room temperature or chilled.

Vegan Mango Quinoa Salad

Salad Ingredients:
1 cup quinoa
2 cups cold water
1/4 tsp salt
1 ripe mango, peeled and chopped
OR: 1/2 cup dried mango slices, soaked overnight, then cut in 1/2 inch dice
1/4 cup blanched slivered or sliced almonds
2 Tbsp roasted pumpkin seeds
1 medium cucumber, peeled and diced

Dressing Ingredients:
2 Tbsp olive oil
1/4 tsp turmeric
Juice of 1 lime
2 Tbsp chopped fresh cilantro
Salt and freshly ground black pepper

Wash quinoa and boil in water for 10 minutes. Cover and let quinoa sit until it absorbs all the water. Fluff quinoa with a fork and let it cool to room temperature

Peel the mango and cut into cubes. Peel and slice the cucumber thinly. Add cucumber to mango along with the almonds and pumpkin seeds

Heat 1 tsp oil in a small pan and fry with turmeric for 30 seconds, then let it cool

Add the lime juice. Mix in olive oil, cilantro, salt and pepper with a whisk or a fork. Add the cooled quinoa to the mango mixture, pour the dressing over the salad, and toss. Serve immediately, or cover and chill

Artichoke Heart And Quinoa Salad

1 cup pecans, toasted
1 cup uncooked quinoa
2 1/2 cups water
2 heads Belgian endive leaves, separated and rinsed
2 cups artichoke hearts, halved, quartered
2 pints cherry or grape tomatoes
2 shallots, thinly sliced

Heat large skillet over medium, and dry-roast pecans, stirring continuously to prevent scorching, until fragrant and slightly browned. Remove from heat and set aside to cool.

Combine quinoa with water in large saucepan, and bring to a boil over medium. Reduce heat to medium-low and continue cooking grains, stirring occasionally, until tender, for 15 to 20 minutes. Scoop quinoa into strainer, rinse under cold water, drain well and set aside.

Meanwhile, layer dinner plates with endive leaves. In separate mixing bowl, combine artichoke hearts, cherry tomatoes and sliced shallots.

When quinoa is cool, stir grain and vegetables together, and dress as desired, tossing to combine. Arrange mixture on endive leaves, garnish with toasted pecans and serve.

Bean-Wah Salad

1/2 cup vegetable broth
1/4 cup quinoa
1 small lemon, juiced
2 tablespoons olive oil
2 tablespoons cilantro or parsley, chopped
2 stalks green onions (scallions) chopped
1 teaspoon minced garlic
1 teaspoon cumin
1 can (15 oz. size) black beans, drained and rinsed
1 tomato, seeded and diced
1 cup fresh or frozen corn (thawed, if frozen)

Cook quinoa in broth about 15 minutes, until liquid is absorbed.

In a large bowl, make the dressing by mixing lemon juice, olive oil, parsley or cilantro, scallions, garlic and cumin.

Add drained and rinsed beans, chopped tomatoes and corn to the bowl. No need to cook the fresh corn; just cut it right off the cobs.

When quinoa is fully cooked and has cooled a bit, add it to the salad and mix everything thoroughly.

Best refrigerated for at least one hour to let flavors mingle, but you can eat it immediately if you're hungry!

Variations: Use bulgur or another grain instead of quinoa. Use lime instead of lemon. Substitute other varieties of beans.

Citrus-Scented Quinoa And Raisin Salad

Balsamic Syrup
1 cup balsamic vinegar
1/4 cup sugar

Salad
1 tablespoon minced garlic
3 tablespoons minced onion
1/2 cup olive oil, divided
8 ounces quinoa
3 cups fresh orange juice
1/2 cup fresh lime juice
1 teaspoon minced fresh thyme
1 cup white wine
1/2 cup natural raisins
1/2 cup toasted almonds
2 teaspoons minced fresh basil
Salt and pepper
1 cup seeded and diced cucumber
1 cup diced ripe plum tomatoes
1 1/2 cup mixed baby greens

For balsamic syrup, combine vinegar and sugar in heavy saucepan and simmer on low until reduced by half. Cool and pour into a plastic squeeze bottle; chill.

For salad, sauté garlic and onion in half the olive oil over low heat in a hot skillet for 1 minute. Add quinoa and sauté 2 minutes longer, stirring constantly.

Stir in orange juice, lime juice, thyme and wine; simmer for 20 minutes, stirring occasionally, until all liquid is absorbed. Remove from heat and let stand for 10 minutes; then, chill thoroughly.

Then, combine chilled quinoa mixture, raisins, almonds, basil and remaining olive oil in large mixing bowl; season lightly with salt and pepper and mix well. For each serving, set a ring mold 4-inches in diameter by 6-inches high on serving plate. Layer ingredients into the mold starting with quinoa salad, then diced cucumber, follow with diced tomatoes, and top off with mixed greens. Remove mold and drizzle plate with balsamic syrup. Repeat until all plates are prepared

Golden Sunshine Quinoa Salad

2 cups quinoa
2 1/2 cups vegetable broth
4 scallions -- light and white green part only, thinly sliced
1/2 cup chopped golden raisins
2 tablespoons rice vinegar
1/2 cup fresh orange juice
1 teaspoon grated orange zest
2 tablespoons extra-virgin olive oil
1/4 teaspoon ground cumin
1 cucumber -- peeled, halved, seeded and chopped
1/2 cup chopped flat-leaf parsley
Salt
Freshly ground black pepper

Place the quinoa in a fine-mesh sieve and rinse under cold water until the water runs clear. Bring the vegetable stock to a boil in a medium saucepan over medium-high heat. Add the quinoa and return to a boil.

Reduce the heat to low, cover, and simmer the quinoa until it has expanded fully, about 20 to 25 minutes. Uncover, fluff with a fork and set aside to cool.

Place the cooled quinoa in a large bowl. Add the scallions, raisins, rice vinegar, orange juice and zest, olive oil, cumin, cucumber and parsley and toss to combine. Season with salt and pepper, to taste, cover with plastic wrap and refrigerate until cold, then serve.

Mediterranean Quinoa

1/2 cup red wine vinegar
2 teaspoons olive oil
2 cloves garlic – minced
2 teaspoons freshly ground pepper
1/2 teaspoon salt
2 medium green bell pepper – chopped
1 cup cucumber – chopped
1/2 cup kalamata olive -- pitted and sliced
1/2 cup red onion – chopped
1/2 cup fresh parsley – chopped
4 cups quinoa -- cooked

In glass jar with tight fitting lid, combine vinegar, oil, garlic, ground pepper and salt. Seal and shake well.

In large bowl, combine bell peppers, cucumber, olives, onion and parsley. Mix well. Add vinegar mixture and toss to coat. Add quinoa, stir gently but thoroughly to combine; serve.

Quinoa And Black Bean Salad

1 1/2 cup quinoa
2 1/4 cups water
1 1/2 cup canned black beans, rinsed and drained
1 1/2 tablespoon red wine vinegar
1 1/2 cup cooked corn (fresh, canned or frozen)
1 red bell pepper, seeded and chopped
4 scallions, chopped
1 teaspoon garlic, minced fine
1/4 teaspoon cayenne pepper
1/4 cup fresh coriander leaves, chopped fine
1/3 cup fresh lime juice
1/2 teaspoon salt
1 1/4 teaspoon ground cumin
1/3 cup olive oil

Rinse quinoa in a fine sieve under cold running water until water runs clear. Put quinoa in a pot with the water. Bring to a boil, then cover and simmer 20 minutes or until water is absorbed and quinoa is tender. Fluff quinoa with a fork and transfer to a large bowl and allow to cool.

While quinoa is cooking, in a small bowl toss beans with vinegar and salt and pepper to taste. Add beans, corn, bell pepper, scallions, garlic, cayenne and coriander to the quinoa. Toss well.

In a small bowl whisk together lime juice, salt, cumin and add oil in a stream while whisking. Drizzle over salad and toss well with salt and pepper. Salad may be made a day ahead and refrigerated, covered. Bring to room temperature before serving.

Quinoa Black Bean Salad

1/3 cup Quinoa
1 cup Water
1 tablespoon Olive oil
4 teaspoons Lime juice
1/4 teaspoon Cumin
1/4 teaspoon Ground coriander
1 tablespoon Fresh cilantro; finely chopped
2 tablespoons Scallions; minced
1 can (15 oz size) Black beans; drained
2 cups Tomatoes; diced
1 cup Bell peppers; diced
2 teaspoons Fresh green chilies; minced
1 dash each salt and pepper; to taste

Rinse the quinoa well in a sieve under cool running water. In a saucepan, bring water to boil, add quinoa, cover, and simmer on low heat until all of the water is absorbed and quinoa is tender, about 10-15 mins. Allow to cool for 15 mins.

In small bowl, combine oil, lime juice, cumin, coriander, cilantro and scallions. Stir in beans, tomatoes, peppers and chiles. Add cooled quinoa, and salt and pepper and combine thoroughly. Refrigerate until ready to serve. Garnish with lemon or lime wedges.

Quinoa Pilaf

1 cup uncooked quinoa, well rinsed
2 1/4 cups vegetable broth
1 small onion, minced
2 tablespoons olive oil
1/4 teaspoon saffron threads
2 cloves garlic, minced
1 teaspoon toasted cumin seeds
1/4 cup red bell pepper, diced
1/4 cup green bell pepper, diced
1 bay leaf
Sea salt and pepper to taste
2 tablespoons fresh cilantro leaves, chopped

Steep saffron in broth for 10 minutes. In a saucepan cook the onion in the oil over moderate heat until softened.

Add the garlic and cumin seeds and cook stirring 1 minute more. Add the broth, quinoa, bell peppers, bay leaf and salt, bring the liquid to a boil and simmer, covered, until the quinoa is soft. Stir in cilantro. Serve.

Quinoa With Summer Veggies

1 cup quinoa
2 cups water
2 vegan bouillon cubes
1 clove garlic, minced
2 medium tomatoes, diced
1 cucumber, peeled and diced
1/2 yellow sweet pepper, diced
1 small red onion, diced
2 tablespoons olive oil
3 tablespoons lemon or lime juice (fresh is best, but bottled will do)
Sea salt to taste

Mix quinoa, water, bouillon, and garlic in a large saucepan and bring to a boil. Lower heat and simmer for about 15 minutes or until all liquid is absorbed.

Remove from heat. Stir in vegetables. Mix oil and juice. Pour over quinoa and vegetables and toss. Serve hot or cold.

Quinoa With Toasted Hazelnuts And Dried Cranberries

1 tablespoon olive oil
1 small onion
1 cup quinoa, rinsed well in cold water
2 cups vegetable broth
1 bay leaf
1 tablespoon ground cinnamon
1/2 cup dried cranberries
1/2 teaspoon salt
1/2 teaspoon fresh ground pepper
1/2 cup sliced hazelnuts
1 tablespoon oil

Heat the olive oil in a sauce pan over medium heat. Add onion and cook, stirring occasionally, until slightly soft. Add quinoa and toast the grains, stirring often, until fragrant and slightly browned.

Stir in broth and bring to a boil over high heat, then reduce heat and simmer. Add bay leave(s) cinnamon, cranberries, salt and pepper. Cook over low heat until all liquid is absorbed, about 15 minutes. Remove pan from heat and stir in nuts and oil. Cover and let stand for 5 minutes before serving.

Red Quinoa Salad

2 cups vegetable, mushroom broth or water
1 clove garlic minced
1 cup Inca Red Quinoa (red variety)
1 small carrot grated
1 tablespoon minced red onion
1/4 cup extra virgin olive oil
1/2 fresh lemon, juiced
2 tablespoons fresh chopped cilantro (or fresh dill or Italian parsley)
salt and pepper to taste

Bring broth or water with garlic to a boil. Add quinoa and cover and simmer low about 10 to 15 minutes or until liquid has been absorbed, Remove from heat and keep pot covered another 10 minutes.

Quinoa should be soft with a translucent color and a white germ ring around the edges of the grain. Usually Quinoa is cooked with ratio one part Quinoa to 2 parts liquid resulting in 4 to 6 servings.

Use cooked quinoa as a side dish, salad, stuffing, filling for tomatoes or vegetables or as a pattie which can be sauté or baked.

For this salad: cool completely or use warm. Mix with remaining ingredients and adjust seasoning to taste. Chill or serve warm or room temperature

Quinoa Lentil Salad

1 cup quinoa
1 cup lentils
1/2 cup mint or basil, chopped
1/2 cup parsley, chopped
4 fat scallions, minced

Dressing:
Zest of two lemons
1/2 cup lemon juice
1/2 cup olive oil
1 tsp paprika
2 tsp garlic, minced
salt and fresh-ground pepper to taste

Simmer quinoa in two cups of water until the water is absorbed, about 20 minutes

Place the lentils in a medium-size pan, cover with at least an inch of water, and boil until tender, 30 to 40 minutes

While the quinoa and lentils are cooking, prepare the dressing, mixing all ingredients. Pour the dressing over the quinoa and lentils while they are hot

Once the salad has cooled, mix in the chopped herbs and scallions

Greek Quinoa and Avocado Salad

1/2 cup uncooked quinoa, rinsed and drained*
1 cup water
2 roma tomatoes, seeded and finely chopped
1/2 cup shredded fresh spinach
1/3 cup finely chopped red onion (1 small)
2 tablespoons lemon juice
2 tablespoons olive oil
1/2 teaspoon salt
Spinach leaves
2 ripe avocados, halved, seeded, peeled, and sliced**

In a 1-1/2-quart saucepan combine quinoa and water. Bring to boiling; reduce heat. Simmer, covered, about 15 minutes or until liquid is absorbed.

Transfer quinoa to a medium bowl. Add tomato, spinach, and onion; stir to combine. In a small bowl, whisk together lemon juice, oil, and salt. Add to quinoa mixture; toss to coat.

Place spinach leaves on 4 salad plates. Arrange avocado slices on spinach leaves. Spoon quinoa mixture over avocado slices. Makes 4 main-dish servings.

Quinoa Salad with Grapes

1 cup quinoa
2 cups water
1/4 cup slivered almonds
1 cup grapes
2 teaspoons fresh marjoram
2 tablespoons verjus
2 tablespoons grapeseed oil
1/8 teaspoon Kosher salt

Rinse and drain quinoa in a fine strainer. Place quinoa and water in a medium saucepan. Bring to a boil over high heat, then reduce heat to low, cover, and simmer for 15-20 minutes, until water is absorbed and quinoa is fluffy. Transfer quinoa to a bowl and cool at least to room temperature.

Toast almonds in a skillet until golden brown (watch them carefully and shake the pan; they will toast quickly!). Set aside to cool.

Cut grapes in half and coarsely chop the marjoram. Set aside.

In a small bowl, whisk together the verjus and grapeseed oil. Add salt and whisk to combine.

Once quinoa has cooled, add grapes, almonds, marjoram, and dressing. Toss to combine.

May be served at room temperature or chilled.

International Quinoa Salad

Quinoa:
1 1/2 cups quinoa, rinsed very well
2 1/4 cups water
1 clove garlic, minced or pressed
1/2 tsp. salt (optional)

Vegetables:
1 large cucumber, peeled, seeded, and diced
2 medium-large tomatoes, finely chopped
kernels of 2 ears of cooked corn (about 1 cup)
1 jalapeño pepper, seeded and diced
1 1/2 cups cooked chickpeas
1/2 cup scallions, thinly sliced
2/3 cup parsley – minced
1/3 cup fresh mint – minced
1 ripe avocado, peeled, pitted, and diced (reserve a few slices for garnish)

Dressing:
1/4 cup freshly squeezed lime juice (NOT lemon)
3 tablespoons vegetable broth or bean cooking liquid
1/2 teaspoon salt, or to taste (optional)
1/8 teaspoon ground pepper
1 clove garlic, pressed or minced
1/4 - 1/2 teaspoon chipotle chili pepper

To cook the quinoa in a pressure cooker, place it and the water, garlic, and salt in the cooker and lock the lid. Over high heat, bring to high pressure and cook for one minute. Remove from heat and allow the pressure to come down naturally. Fluff the quinoa and allow it to cool.

Combine all of the vegetables in a large bowl. Add the quinoa and mix well. Whisk the dressing ingredients together and pour over the salad. Mix well and refrigerate until chilled. Taste before serving, and add more lime juice as necessary (you want it to be tangy). Garnish with avocado slices and serve. Makes about 10 servings

Chapter 4 - Vegan Quinoa Soup

Quinoa, Sauerkraut & Bean Soup

6 Eden Whole Shiitake Mushrooms
15 ounces Pinto Beans, do not drain or Kidney Beans
1 Tablespoon Toasted Sesame Oil
3 cloves garlic, pressed or minced
1 cup onion, chopped
4 cups water, including reserved shiitake soaking water
1 2/3 cup Sauerkraut, rinsed, drained, chopped
1/4 cup Quinoa, washed and drained
2 teaspoons paprika powder
1 Tablespoon Soy Sauce, or to taste
1/4 teaspoon black pepper, freshly ground
2 Tablespoons fresh parsley, minced

Soak shiitake mushrooms in 1 cup hot water for 20 minutes or until soft. Drain and save soaking water. Discard stems and slice mushroom caps.

Puree beans in a blender or food processor and set aside.

Heat oil and sauté garlic and onions until onions are translucent. Add 3 cups water, shiitake mushrooms with soaking liquid, sauerkraut, and quinoa. Cook 30 minutes over low heat.

Add paprika, soy sauce, pureed beans, and black pepper. Simmer for 5 to 10 minutes.

Quinoa Corn Soup

1 Tablespoon Safflower Oil
1 clove garlic, minced
2 teaspoons cumin seed or 1 teaspoon ground cumin
6 cups water or vegetable broth
1 large carrot, halved lengthwise and sliced
1/2 cup Quinoa, washed and drained
3 cups sweet corn, fresh or frozen
1/4 teaspoon cayenne pepper
1 teaspoon Sea Salt, or to taste
15 ounces Pinto Beans, do not drain
1/2 cup fresh parsley, coarsely chopped
1 Tablespoon lime juice, freshly squeezed

In a large soup pot, heat the oil. Sauté the garlic and cumin for 1 minute, stirring frequently. Add the stock and bring to a boil.

Add the carrot, quinoa, corn, cayenne and sea salt.

Cover and return to a boil. Lower the heat and simmer for 10 minutes. Add the beans and continue to simmer for 10 minutes.

Just before serving, stir in the parsley and enough lime juice to make the flavors pop.

Quinoa Vegetable Soup

1 tablespoon vegetable oil
2/3 cup quinoa
1 carrot, diced
1 stalk celery, diced
1/2 onion, finely chopped
1/2 green bell pepper, seeded and chopped
2 cloves garlic, crushed
4 cups vegetable broth
3 1/2 cups water
2 large tomatoes, finely chopped
1/4 head cabbage, chopped
salt and pepper to taste
1/4 cup chopped fresh parsley, for garnish

Heat the vegetable oil in a large pot on medium-high heat. Stir in the quinoa, carrot, celery, onion, bell pepper, and garlic. Cook for a few minutes, until lightly browned, stirring frequently

Pour in the vegetable broth, water, tomatoes, and cabbage. Increase heat to high and bring to a boil. Reduce heat to medium and simmer until the quinoa and vegetables are tender, about 10 minutes.

Season to taste with salt and pepper. Garnish with parsley

Carrot Top & Quinoa Soup

1 tablespoon light olive oil or canola oil
1/2 sweet onion, diced
4 cups water
4 medium carrots, peeled and cut into 1/4 inch rounds
1 cup carrot, tops washed and finely chopped
1/2 cup quinoa, rinsed
sea salt
fresh ground black pepper

In a 3-quart pot, sauté the onion in oil until translucent, then add the remaining ingredients and simmer for 20-25 minutes. Season with salt and pepper.

Quinoa Soup with Corn

1 (14.5 oz) can vegetable broth
1/2 c quinoa, rinsed and drained
1 3/4 c water
1/4 tsp cayenne pepper
2 cloves garlic, minced
1 c frozen or fresh corn kernels
1 1/2 Tbsp chopped parsley or cilantro
1 Tbsp fresh lime juice

Rinse quinoa well in a fine strainer.

Place broth, quinoa, water, cayenne and garlic in a small soup pot and bring to a boil. Reduce heat to medium and cook 10 minutes.

Add corn kernels and cook 3 minutes. Add parsley or cilantro and cook for 1 minute. Remove from heat and stir in the lime juice. Serve hot or cold.

Curried Sweet Potato and Quinoa Soup

1 tbsp vegetable oil
2 onions, finely chopped
2 carrots, peeled and diced
2 stalks celery, diced
2 cloves garlic, minced
2 tsp minced gingerroot
2 tsp curry powder
1 tsp freshly grated orange zest
2 cups sweet potato purée (see Tip)
6 cups reduced-sodium vegetable stock
3/4 cup quinoa
1 cup freshly squeezed orange juice
1/4 cup pure maple syrup
Salt and freshly ground black pepper
Toasted chopped walnuts or sliced almonds

In a large saucepan or stockpot, heat oil over medium heat for 30 seconds. Add onions, carrots and celery and cook, stirring, until carrots have softened, about 7 minutes.

Add garlic, ginger, curry powder and orange zest and cook, stirring, for 1 minute. Add sweet potato and stock and stir well. Bring to a boil. Stir in quinoa. Reduce heat to low. Cover and simmer until quinoa is tender and flavors have blended, about 30 minutes.

Add orange juice and maple syrup and heat through. Season to taste with salt and pepper. Ladle into bowls and garnish with toasted.

Tip: To get this quantity of puréed sweet potato, bake, peel and mash 2 medium sweet potatoes, each about 6 oz. You can also use a can (14 oz) of sweet potato purée.

QUINOA SOUP WITH AVOCADO AND CORN

4 cups vegetable broth
1 cup quinoa
1 cup frozen corn kernels
1/3 cup chunky salsa, to taste
1 ripe but firm Hass avocado, diced
Salt
1/4 cup chopped fresh cilantro
Lime wedges, for serving

In a large saucepan over high heat, bring the broth to a boil. Stir in the quinoa, reduce heat to medium-high, and continue boiling, uncovered, for 15 minutes.

Stir in the corn and salsa, then return to a simmer. Remove the pan from the heat and stir in the avocado. Season with salt and stir in the cilantro. Ladle into large bowls, accompanied with lime wedges.

Eggplant Quinoa Soup

1-4 T EVOO
1 large onion, diced
8 cloves garlic, pressed
1/2 t red pepper flakes
2 t dried basil
1 t dried marjoram
1/2 t fennel seeds
1/2 t dried rosemary
pinch salt/pinch pepper
2 T balsamic vinegar
1 medium eggplant, diced
3 c white bean of choice (29 oz can)
8 c water or vegetable stock (plus vegetable bouillon cube if using water)
28 oz canned tomato (crushed, sauce, stewed, or whole)
1/2 c quinoa
Salt/Pepper to taste
Fresh Basil (optional, but VERY good)
Baby Spinach (optional)
1 t EVOO and 1 T nutritional yeast per bowl for finishing

In a heavy bottomed 4 quart pot over medium heat add the oil, onions, dried spices and a pinch salt/pepper. Sauté for several minutes then add garlic. When the onions are translucent, deglaze with vinegar.

Add the eggplant, beans and water or stock, tomatoes. Bring to a boil for several minutes, then turn heat down to low, cover and simmer for 30 minutes.

Turn off heat, add quinoa, around a cup of fresh basil and cover for 20 minutes. Taste and adjust seasonings.

Serve with more fresh basil, baby spinach and a teaspoon of evoo.

Quinoa Pumpkin Soup

1 T olive oil
1 onion, chopped (about 3/4-1 C)
a few cloves of garlic, sliced thin
1 C Quinoa
1 C pumpkin, small dice
1 C fresh (or frozen) sweet corn
2 C shredded fresh spinach
1 green pepper, small dice
salt and pepper
4-5 C water
2 t soy sauce
dash of ground habanero chili (optional)

Heat oil in a heavy pan and add the chopped onion. Stir, season with salt and pepper, and brown on medium heat (about 8-10 minutes).

Add the sliced garlic and stir another two minutes. Add the pumpkin (or any other squash of your choice), and stir for a minute.

Add 3 cups of water and bring to boil. Add quinoa, bring to boil again. Simmer and cook covered for 15 minutes. Add corn and cook 5 minutes, adding more water.

Now add the spinach in handfuls and cook a further 5 minutes. Add soy sauce and simmer a couple of minute to blend flavors. You can add more pepper, or any chili powder of your choice

Quinoa Soup with Spinach and Tomatoes

1 teaspoon olive oil
1/2 red onion, minced
2 small cloves garlic, minced
1 teaspoon salt
1/4 teaspoon freshly ground black pepper
2 sprigs fresh rosemary, leaves chopped
4 cups water (or vegetable broth)
2 vegetable bouillon cubes (can omit if using broth)
1 cup quinoa, rinsed
1 14.5 oz can chopped tomatoes
1 6 oz package of fresh baby spinach, chopped

Heat olive oil in large sauce pan, add red onion and sauté until onions are transparent. Add garlic, salt, pepper, and rosemary, and heat for a minute or so.

Add water and vegetable bouillon and bring to a boil. Add quinoa and simmer for 15 minutes. Add tomatoes and simmer for another 5 minutes. Add spinach and simmer for another minute or so. Serve immediately.

African Quinoa Soup with Vegetables

2 tbs oil
1 med chopped onion
2 garlic cloves, minced
1 sm fresh jalapeno, minced OR 1 tbs canned diced green chilies, up to 2 T
1 red bell pepper, diced
2 diced celery stalks, with leaves
2 med diced zucchini
1 med sweet potato, diced
1 tsp ground cumin
1 tsp dried oregano
6 cup vegetable stock
½ cup quinoa
salt and pepper to taste
1 dash cayenne pepper
½ cup chunky organic, natural peanut butter

Wear rubber gloves to prepare fresh jalapeno pepper.

In a large heavy-bottomed soup pot, heat oil over medium-high heat.

When oil is hot and bubbly, add onion, garlic, jalapeno pepper, bell pepper, celery, zucchini, sweet potato, cumin and oregano.

Sauté 10 -15 minutes, or until vegetables are softened. Add stock, quinoa, black pepper and cayenne pepper.

Bring to a boil, reduce heat and cover. Simmer until quinoa is cooked and vegetables are tender, about 10 to 15 minutes.

Add peanut butter, using a wooden spoon to blend in completely, and simmer another 10 minutes. Taste, and adjust seasonings.

Quinoa, Leek and Potato Soup in a Slow Cooker

2 very large leeks
1 onion
2 large potatoes
1 cup quinoa
2 pints vegetable stock
salt and pepper to taste
olive oil

Warm up your slow cooker for 20 minutes on high setting

Slice the leeks and potatoes.

Chop the onion

Fry these ingredients in a large wok for 2 minutes

Add the stock and salt and pepper

Bring the mix to the boil

Add the quinoa and bring back to the boil

Transfer the soup to the slow cooker.

Cook on low setting for 5 – 6 hours.

Just before serving purify the soup for 20 seconds.

Serve on its own or with croutons

Quinoa Cabbage Soup

2 to 3 tablespoons extra virgin olive oil
1 very large sweet onion, cut into crescent moons
2 to 3 cloves garlic, crushed
1 to 2 teaspoons grated fresh ginger
4 large carrots cut into matchsticks
6 cups water
2 to 3 teaspoon Herb mare (or to taste)
2 cups cooked quinoa
2 cups (or more) sliced savoy cabbage
1/2 cup chopped cilantro
freshly ground black pepper to taste

Heat a 6-quart pot over medium heat. Add the olive oil. Then add the onions. Sauté for 10 to 15 minutes.

Make sure your heat isn't' too high or your onions will brown too much and cause the broth to be off in flavor. Just a steady, medium heat so the onions soften and cook is all that is needed.

Add the garlic, ginger and carrots and sauté 5 minutes more. Add the water, Herb mare, and cooked quinoa and simmer for about 10 to 15 minutes or until carrots reach desired tenderness. Add in cabbage and cook a few more minutes; this doesn't take long.

Turn off heat and add the cilantro and freshly ground black pepper. Taste and add more Herb mare and/or pepper if needed. Stir it all together and serve!

LENTIL SOUP WITH CHICKPEAS AND QUINOA

1/2 a red onion diced
A splash of sunflower oil
1 clove of garlic chopped
a small knob of grated ginger
1 tsp each of ground cumin, coriander, chilies and turmeric
1/2 tsp of ground cloves
1 cup of red lentils
2-3 cups of vegetable stock
1 can of chickpeas aka garbanzo beans
1 cup of cooked quinoa
salt and pepper to taste
chopped coriander to garnish
squeeze of lime juice

Heat the oil in a thick bottomed saucepan and fry off the onions on a medium heat.

Add the ground spices and stir until it becomes aromatic. Add the garlic and ginger and stir again for a few minutes. Add the red lentils and toss in the spice mixture for one minute

Add the veggie stock and cook on high heat till it comes to a rapid boil. Lower the heat and let the ingredients simmer for about 10-15 mins. Season to taste

Remove from the heat and blend using a stab blender or do it manually using a regular blender. Add the drained and rinsed chickpeas and let it simmer for another 5 mins

Take off the heat and stir through the cooked quinoa. Squeeze a little lime juice. Garnish with chopped coriander. The soup is best served hot.

Quinoa and Tomato Soup

1 Tablespoon(s) Unrefined oil
1 Teaspoon(s) Fresh cilantro; minced
1 Garlic clove; pressed
1 Onion; diced
1/2 Green pepper; chopped
2 Celery stalks; chopped
1 Cup(s) Tomato; chopped
6 Cup(s) Vegetable Stock
1/2 Cup(s) Quinoa

Heat a 2-qt. soup pot.

Add oil and sauté cilantro, garlic, onion, pepper, celery and then tomato. Add salt and pepper. Add stock and bring to a boil. Add quinoa and return to a boil.

Cover, reduce heat and simmer for 45 minutes. Garnish each bowl with scallions. Serve hot

African Quinoa Peanut Soup

3/4 cup quinoa, rinsed
3 tablespoons olive oil
1 medium onion, chopped small
1 red bell pepper, diced small
2 celery stalks, diced small
2 medium sweet potatoes, diced 1 inch pieces (about 3 cups)
1 large jalapeno, deseeded and deveined, diced small
1/4 teaspoon crushed red pepper flakes
2 small zucchini, diced 1 ½ inches
4 cloves garlic, minced
1 1/2 teaspoons ground cumin
1 1/2 teaspoons dried oregano
1/2 teaspoon black pepper
1 1/2 teaspoons salt
8 cups water
1 cup chunky peanut butter (fresh ground or jarred – natural without sweeteners/oil)
2 cups frozen or fresh okra, optional

In a small bowl, rinse quinoa until water runs clear. Prepare and measure out all remaining ingredients in advance. Heat a Dutch oven or large heavy-bottomed pot on medium-high heat; add oil and onion, red bell pepper, celery, sweet potatoes, jalapeno and red pepper flakes. Sauté for 15 minutes or until sweet potatoes are slightly soft.

Next add zucchini, minced garlic, cumin, oregano, pepper and salt; sauté 2 to 3 minutes, careful not to burn garlic. Add 8 cups water; deglaze pot with a wooden spoon. Add quinoa (rinsed and drained). Bring to a boil, cover and reduce heat, simmer 15 minutes or until quinoa is cooked.

Remove about 1 1/2 cups of hot liquid from the soup, pour into a small bowl. Add peanut butter to small bowl, use a wooden spoon or a whisk to blend and make a thin paste. (This step prevents clumping.) Pour peanut paste into the soup, and mix well. If using okra, add now. Simmer 5 – 10 minutes. Taste and adjust seasonings. Serve hot, topped with a few rough chopped peanuts

Quinoa Soup with Spinach and Corn

2 tbs. olive oil, divided
1 lb. mushrooms, sliced (use white, Portobello, or a combination)
salt and freshly ground black pepper to taste
1 large red or white onion, chopped
6 cloves garlic, thinly sliced
1 3/4 cups quinoa
8 cups vegetable broth
3 cups water
2 cups frozen or fresh corn
12-14 oz. spinach leaves
2 tbs. soy sauce

Heat 1 tbs. of the oil in a large pot over medium-high heat. Add the mushrooms, season with salt and pepper and cook, stirring often, until the water they release nearly evaporates, about 5 minutes.

Reduce heat to medium-low and continue cooking until lightly browned and soft. Remove to a bowl and set aside.

Add the remaining oil to the pot and heat to medium. Add the onions, season and cook until soft and browned, about 8 minutes. Add the garlic, cook for 2 minutes more and add the vegetable broth.

Cover and bring to a boil, then add the quinoa. Reduce heat to low and simmer, covered, for 15 minutes. Uncover and add the water and corn and return to a simmer. Add the spinach leaves a few handfuls at a time.

Add the reserved mushrooms and soy sauce. Simmer for a few minutes to blend the flavors, taste for seasoning and add more salt and pepper as needed.

Thick Lentil Soup with Quinoa and Spinach

1 cup of black French lentils
1/2 cup quinoa
1 bunch of fresh spinach (about 3 cups or about half a package of frozen spinach, thawed)
2 small onions cut to small dice
4 medium carrots cut to small dice
2 cloves of garlic
3 tablespoons of olive oil
1 tablespoon of ground cumin
Juice from half a lemon
2 cups vegetable broth
4 cups of water
Salt and pepper

Put the onion in a big pot with the olive oil and a bit of salt on medium low heat and sweat for about 10 minutes without browning.

Add the carrots and sauté for another 10 minutes. The veggies should become soft and sweet. Add garlic, cumin and lentils and sauté for a minute while mixing.

Add the broth and the water, bring to a boil, lower the heat and cook for 30 minutes. Add the quinoa and salt and pepper, bring to a boil, lower the heat and cook for another 15 minutes until the quinoa is soft and kind of translucent.

Check from time to time if the soup looks to think for your liking you can add 1/2 cup of water (though it suppose to be a thick soup, like a stew). Lightly chop the spinach if you're not using baby spinach. Add to the pot and cook for few more minutes and take off the heat and add the lemon and taste for salt and pepper, add if necessary. You can serve with a drizzle of good sharp olive oil

Crockpot Quinoa Red Lentil Soup

1/2 cup quinoa
3/4 cup small red lentils
Optional: 2 Tbsp olive oil
2 large carrots
2 stalks celery
1 small head cauliflower OR 2 medium potatoes or 1 med. zucchini OR 1 small butternut squash
1 bay leaf
2 inch piece cinnamon stick
2 thin slices fresh ginger
1/2 jalapeno pepper, seeded
6 cups water or vegetable stock
1/2 tsp cumin
1/2 tsp fennel seed
1/2 tsp turmeric
1/2 tsp paprika
1/2 tsp coriander
1/2 tsp dried thyme leaf or 1 sprig fresh
1 tsp dried basil or 1 Tbsp minced fresh
1/4 tsp dried rosemary leaves or 1 sprig fresh
1 tsp salt or to taste and fresh ground black pepper
4 Tbsp minced fresh herbs: parsley, cilantro or basil
Optional: 2 cups chopped fresh greens: kale, chard, or spinach
More Heat: Add 1/2 - 1 tsp green curry paste OR 1/4 tsp cayenne powder

Rinse the quinoa and red lentils in a bowl or pan, then drain into a colander. Peel the carrots, slice lengthwise, then slice in thin pieces

Wash and trim the celery stalks, then slice crosswise in thin pieces. Break or cut the cauliflower into large chunks - these will break up into smaller pieces as they cook

Combine olive oil, quinoa, lentils, herbs & spices, fresh ginger and jalapeno in the crockpot, and cover with the 6 cups water

Cover and cook on low for 6 hours or more if needed. 20 minutes before serving, turn the heat up to high and stir in optional greens

Just before serving, add the minced fresh parsley, basil or cilantro, salt & pepper, and serve, removing the ginger slices, bay leaves, cinnamon stick, as you come across them

Chapter 5 - Vegan Quinoa Main Dish

Quinoa with Moroccan Winter Squash and Carrot Stew

2 tablespoons olive oil
1 cup chopped onion
3 garlic cloves, chopped
2 teaspoons Hungarian sweet paprika
1 teaspoon salt
1/2 teaspoon ground black pepper
1/2 teaspoon ground coriander
1/2 teaspoon ground cumin
1/2 teaspoon turmeric
1/2 teaspoon ground ginger
1/2 teaspoon cayenne pepper
Pinch of saffron
1 cup water
1 14 1/2-ounce can diced tomatoes, drained
2 tablespoons fresh lemon juice
3 cups 1-inch cubes peeled butternut squash (from 1 1/2-pound squash)
2 cups 3/4-inch cubes peeled carrots

For Quinoa
1 cup quinoa*
2 tablespoon olive oil
1/2 cup finely chopped onion
1/4 cup finely chopped peeled carrot
2 garlic cloves, minced
1/2 teaspoon salt
1/2 teaspoon turmeric
2 cups water
1/2 cup chopped fresh cilantro, divided
2 teaspoons chopped fresh mint, divided

For stew:

Heat oil in large saucepan over medium heat. Add onion; sauté until soft, stirring often, about 5 minutes. Add garlic; stir 1 minute. Mix in paprika and next 8 ingredients. Add 1 cup water, tomatoes, and lemon juice. Bring to boil. Add squash and carrots. Cover and simmer over medium-low heat until vegetables are tender, stirring occasionally, about 20 minutes. Season with salt and pepper. (Can be prepared 1 day ahead. Cover and chill.)

For quinoa:

Rinse quinoa; drain. Heat oil in large saucepan over medium heat. Add onion and carrot. Cover; cook until vegetables begin to brown, stirring often, about 10 minutes. Add garlic, salt, and turmeric; sauté 1 minute. Add quinoa; stir 1 minute. Add 2 cups water. Bring to boil; reduce heat to medium-low. Cover; simmer until liquid is absorbed and quinoa is tender, about 15 minutes.

Rewarm stew. Stir in half of cilantro and half of mint. Spoon quinoa onto platter, forming well in center. Spoon stew into well. Sprinkle remaining herbs over.

Black Bean and Quinoa Chili

1 cup quinoa (rinsed)
2 cups water
1 tablespoon oil
1 onion (chopped)
4 cloves garlic (chopped)
1 jalapeno pepper (chopped)
1 tablespoon chili powder
1 tablespoon cumin (toasted and ground)
1 28 ounce can crushed tomatoes
2 19 ounce cans black beans (drained and rinsed)
1 green bell pepper (cut into bit sized pieces)
1 red bell pepper (cut into bit sized pieces)
1 zucchini (cut into bit sized pieces, optional)
1 tablespoon chipotle chili in adobo sauce (chopped)
1 teaspoon dried oregano
salt and pepper to taste
1 cup corn (fresh, frozen or canned)
1 handful cilantro (chopped)

Simmer the quinoa in the water until absorbed, about 20 minutes. Heat the oil in a pan.

Add the onions and sauté until tender, about 3-5 minutes. Add the garlic, chili powder and cumin and sauté until fragrant, about 1 minutes.

Add the tomatoes, beans, peppers, zucchini, chipotle, oregano, salt and pepper and simmer for 20 minutes. Add the quinoa and corn and simmer for 5 minutes. Remove from the heat and stir in the cilantro.

Quinoa Primavera

1 cup quinoa
2 cups water
salt
2 tablespoons extra-virgin olive oil
3 garlic cloves, minced
1 small carrot, cut into 1/4-inch dice (1/2 cup)
1 celery stalk, cut into 1/4-inch dice (1/2 cup)
1/2 red bell pepper, finely diced (1/2 cup)
1/2 green bell pepper, finely diced (1/2 cup)
1/2 cup edamame (or substitute with fresh or frozen peas)
2 scallions, white part only, thinly sliced
fresh ground black pepper
1/4 cup parsley, chopped

Heat a small saucepan over medium-low heat. Add the quinoa and cook, stirring constantly for about 5 minutes (grains should be dry and fragrant). Then add the water and 1/2 teaspoon of salt, cover, simmer and let cook for about 15 minutes or until the quinoa is tender. Do NOT stir the quinoa while simmering.

Combine olive oil and garlic in a large skillet and place it over medium heat. When the oil is hot and garlic is aromatic add the carrots and sauté for 1 minute. Stir in the celery, peppers, edamame (or peas), and scallions.

Sauté just long enough for the veggies to heat through, about 1-2 minutes. Stir in the hot quinoa and season to taste with salt and black pepper...stir in parsley and serve immediately.

Three Bean & Quinoa Chili

2 Tablespoons Extra Virgin Olive Oil
2 cloves garlic, minced
1 large onion, diced
30 ounces Kidney Beans, do not drain
15 ounces Pinto Beans, do not drain
15 ounces Garbanzo Beans, do not drain
1/4 cup Quinoa, rinsed and drained
1/2 cup sweet corn, fresh or frozen
1/2 cup celery, diced
28 ounces Whole Tomatoes with Basil, do not drain, chopped
1 jalapeno pepper, diced
2 cups vegetable stock or water
1 Tablespoon chili powder, or to taste
1 teaspoon Sea Salt,

Heat the oil in a large soup pot and sauté the garlic and onion for 3 minutes. Add the pepper and sauté another 2 minutes.

Add all remaining ingredients, cover and bring to a boil. Reduce the flame to medium low and simmer 35 minutes, stirring occasionally. Adjust the seasoning by adding more chili powder and sea salt, if desired and simmer another 5 minutes.

Serve hot with organic corn chips or crackers.

Spicy Quinoa and Pintos

15 ounces Spicy Pinto Beans, drained and reserve liquid
1 cup Quinoa, washed and drained
1 1/4 cups cold water, including reserved bean cooking water
1 Tablespoon Extra Virgin Olive Oil
1 Tablespoon lime juice, freshly squeezed
2 teaspoons Soy Sauce, or to taste
1 cup roasted red peppers, diced
1/2 cup red onion, finely minced
1/2 cup fresh parsley, chopped fine or fresh cilantro

Pour the bean cooking liquid into a measuring cup and add enough cold water to equal 1-1/4 cups of liquid. Place the liquid in a medium saucepan and bring to a boil. Add the quinoa, cover and simmer for 12 to 15 minutes until the quinoa is tender and fluffy.

While the quinoa is cooking, blend the oil, lime juice and soy sauce in a bowl. Toss in the beans and set aside. When the quinoa is done, toss in with the beans, onions, roasted red pepper, onion and parsley. Mix well and serve warm or room temperature.

Spanish Quinoa

14 1/2 ounces Diced Tomatoes w/Green Chilies, drained, reserve liquid
1 Tablespoon Extra Virgin Olive Oil
3 cloves garlic, pressed
1 medium onion, diced
1/2 cup Quinoa, washed and drained
1 medium green bell pepper, diced
1/2 teaspoon chili powder, or to taste
1 teaspoon ground cumin, optional
1 pinch Sea Salt
1 cup water, including reserved tomato liquid

Drain tomatoes and reserve juice. Heat oil and sauté the onions and garlic until translucent. Place the tomato juice in a measuring cup.

Add enough water to equal 1 cup liquid. Add the liquid to the sautéed vegetables and bring to a boil. Stir in the quinoa, peppers and salt. Cover and cook 15 minutes or until liquid is gone. Stir in tomatoes and spices.

Cook another 2 to 4 minutes until hot. Serve.

Quinoa with Spicy Pintos

15 ounces Spicy Pinto Beans, 1 can, drained, reserve liquid or Chili Beans
1 cup Quinoa, rinsed
1 1/2 cups water, including reserved bean liquid
1 Tablespoon Extra Virgin Olive Oil
1 Tablespoon lime juice, freshly squeezed
1 teaspoon Soy Sauce
1 cup roasted red peppers, diced
1/2 cup fresh parsley, minced or fresh cilantro
1/2 cup red onion, minced

Place 1 1/2 cups of water, including bean juice, in a saucepan, and bring to a boil. Add quinoa, cover, and simmer 15 minutes, until tender.

While the quinoa is cooking, blend the oil, lime juice, and soy sauce in a bowl or blender. Place the beans in a bowl, pour the liquid over, toss, and let sit at room temperature until the quinoa is done.

Add the quinoa, onion, red pepper, and parsley or cilantro. Mix well. Serve warm, room temperature or chilled.

Quinoa with Spicy Chili Beans

15 ounces Chili Beans (seasoned dark red kidney), drained, reserve liquid
1 cup Quinoa, rinsed and drained
1 1/2 cups water, including drained bean liquid
1 Tablespoon Extra Virgin Olive Oil
1 Tablespoon lime juice, freshly squeezed
1 cup roasted red peppers, diced
1/2 cup red onion, finely minced
1/2 cup fresh parsley, finely chopped or fresh cilantro
2 teaspoons Soy Sauce, or to taste

Drain the beans and reserve the liquid in a measuring cup. Add enough cold water to equal 1 1/2 cups of liquid. Place the liquid in a medium saucepan and bring to a boil. Add the quinoa, cover and simmer for 12 to 15 minutes until the quinoa is tender and fluffy.

While the quinoa is cooking, blend the oil, lime juice and soy sauce in a bowl. Toss in the beans and set aside. When the quinoa is done, toss in with the beans. Add onions, roasted red pepper and parsley. Mix well and serve warm or room temperature.

Quinoa Stuffed Red Peppers

4 medium red bell peppers, sliced in half lengthwise and seeded
4 cups water, for blanching peppers
1 cup Quinoa, washed and drained
1 1/4 cups water, for boiling quinoa
1 pinch Eden Sea Salt
1 Tablespoon Extra Virgin Olive Oil
3 cloves garlic, minced
1 cup red onion, minced
1/2 cup golden seedless raisins or coarsely chopped apricots
15 ounces Garbanzo Beans, drained
1/2 teaspoon ground cinnamon
1 teaspoon ground cumin
2 teaspoons Soy Sauce
2 Tablespoons fresh chives, finely chopped for garnish or green onions

Place the quinoa, 1 1/4 cups water and sea salt in a sauce pan, cover and bring to a boil. Simmer on low for 20 minutes.

Remove and place in a mixing bowl. Bring 4 cups water to a boil. Blanch the pepper halves for 2 to 3 minutes. Remove, drain and set aside. Preheat the oven to 350°. Heat oil in a skillet. Sauté the garlic and onions for 1 minute.

Add the raisins, beans, cinnamon, cumin and shoyu. Sauté another 2 minutes. Combine with the quinoa and mix thoroughly. Stuff each pepper half. Place in an oiled baking dish with a little water. Bake for 10 to 15 minutes or until peppers are tender. Remove and garnish with chives.

Quinoa Stuffed Acorn Squash

2 cups Quinoa, leftover, cooked
2 Tablespoons fresh parsley, minced
1 teaspoon Extra Virgin Olive Oil
3 cloves garlic, minced
2 medium acorn squash, halved and seeded
15 ounces Black Eyed Peas, 1 can, rinsed and drained
1/4 cup sunflower seeds, dry, pan roasted
1/4 cup red bell pepper, finely diced
1/4 cup celery, finely diced
2 teaspoons lemon juice, freshly squeezed
2 teaspoons Soy Sauce
1 Tablespoon Safflower Oil, for oiling the squash skin

Directions

Preheat oven to 350°. Mix together, in a medium bowl, the quinoa, parsley, garlic, black eyed peas, sunflower seeds, red pepper, celery, lemon juice and soy sauce. Lightly oil the squash skin, with Safflower Oil, to prevent splitting.

Stuff each squash half with the quinoa stuffing. Sprinkle 1/2 teaspoon lemon juice over each stuffed squash. Place on a baking sheet, cover with foil and bake for 45 minutes or until the squash is tender.

Quinoa Jambalaya

1 teaspoon Hot Pepper Sesame Oil
1 teaspoon Toasted Sesame Oil
1 Tablespoon whole wheat flour
1 medium onion
1 clove garlic, minced
1/2 cup carrots, chopped
1 teaspoon crushed bay leaves or 1 whole bay leaf
1/2 teaspoon dried thyme
1/2 teaspoon Sea Salt
1 1/4 cup vegetable broth or water
1 cup Quinoa, washed and drained
1 medium green bell pepper, diced
1/2 cup fresh parsley, chopped
1 cup celery, chopped
1/2 cup green onion, thinly sliced
6 pieces Dried Tofu, soaked 10 minutes in warm water to cover
14 1/2 ounces Diced Tomatoes w/Green Chilies, drained
1/8 teaspoon freshly ground black pepper, or to to taste

Heat oil in a heavy saucepan. Add flour and stir until a fragrant aroma is released, about 3 minutes. Add onion, garlic, bay leaf, thyme and salt. Slowly add water or vegetable broth, stirring constantly.

Bring to a boil. Squeeze out water from the dried tofu. Rinse under cold water, squeeze again and cube the tofu. Add quinoa, green pepper, parsley, carrots, celery, dried tofu and green onion to the saucepan.

Cover and cook on medium-low heat for 20 minutes. Turn off heat, add tomatoes and let sit, covered, for 10 minutes. Add black pepper to taste. Mix well and serve.

Quinoa Casserole

1 cup Quinoa, washed and drained
1 1/3 cups water
1 teaspoon Hot Pepper Sesame Oil
1 medium onion, chopped
1 clove garlic, pressed
2 teaspoons curry powder, optional
1 cup celery, chopped
2 cups broccoli, chopped
1 medium tomato, chopped
1 Tablespoon Soy Sauce, or to taste
2 Tablespoons Brown Rice Vinegar

Preheat oven to 350°. Roast rinsed quinoa in a dry skillet until it pops, stirring constantly to evenly roast and prevent burning.

Place quinoa in a casserole dish and add the water. Heat oil, sauté onions, garlic and curry in skillet until onions are translucent. Add celery, broccoli and tomato. Sauté briefly and add to quinoa. Add soy sauce and vinegar.

Mix, cover casserole dish and bake for 45 minutes.

Quinoa Black Soybean Tabbouleh

1 cup Quinoa, washed and drained
1 1/2 cups water
1 cup sweet corn, fresh or frozen
3 Tablespoons Extra Virgin Olive Oil
1/3 cup lemon juice, freshly squeezed
30 ounces Black Soybeans, 2 cans, drained
1 teaspoon Soy Sauce
1 cup fresh parsley, minced
1/2 cup red onion, minced
1/3 cup fresh mint leaves, chopped or fresh basil

Place quinoa, corn and water in a sauce pan. Cover and cook for 15 to 20 minutes. Remove and fluff to cool. Combine oil, lemon juice, soysauce and black soybeans.

Marinate 10 minutes. Mix quinoa, soybean mixture and remaining ingredients. Serve.

Quick Quinoa & Bean Stew

1 Tablespoon Extra Virgin Olive Oil
1 cup onion, diced
1/2 cup carrots, diced
15 ounces Navy Beans, do not drain
15 ounces Kidney Beans, do not drain
2 cups vegetable stock
1/2 cup Quinoa, rinsed and drained
1/2 teaspoon Sea Salt, if desired
2 cups baby spinach leaves

Heat oil in a medium soup pot and sauté the onion for 3 to 5 minutes. Add all remaining ingredients except the spinach, cover and bring to a boil.

Reduce the flame to medium-low and simmer for 12 until the quinoa is done. Mix in the spinach greens and cook 1 minute until they are wilted. Remove and serve.

Asian Organic Quinoa with Black Soybeans

15 ounces Black Soybeans, drained, reserve liquid
1 1/2 teaspoons Soy Sauce
1 1/2 cups water, (approx), including reserved bean liquid
1/3 cup snow peas
1 1/3 cups Quinoa, washed and drained
1/2 cup scallions, sliced, keep white and green pars separate
2 large cloves garlic, minced
1/2 cup roasted red peppers, finely diced
1 teaspoon Hot Pepper Sesame Oil
2 teaspoons Toasted Sesame Oil
1 teaspoon Brown Rice Vinegar

Combine the soybeans and 1 teaspoon soy sauce in a small bowl. Let sit several minutes, stirring the beans occasionally. Add enough water to the drained soybean liquid to equal 2 cups. In a heavy saucepan, bring the liquid to a boil.

Blanch the snow peas for 30 seconds. Remove with a slotted spoon. Place in a colander, and run under cold water. Set aside. Add the quinoa, sliced white scallion bulbs, garlic, and the remaining 1/2 teaspoon soy sauce to the boiling water.

Cover and cook over medium heat until the quinoa is tender but still crunchy, about 20 minutes.

While the quinoa is cooking, thinly slice the snow peas and set them in a large serving bowl. Add the beans, red peppers, and sliced scallion greens. Toss in the cooked quinoa and drizzle on the sesame oils and rice vinegar.

Add more soy sauce, to taste, if desired. Serve warm over steamed kale or at room temperature on a bed of watercress or radicchio.

Baked Squash Stuffed with Quinoa & Dried Fruit

2 cups any precooked, Quinoa
2 medium acorn squash, halved and seeded
1/2 cup walnuts, chopped
1/2 cup Dried Cherries, 1 package, coarsely chopped Dried Cranberries, or Dried Wild Blueberries
2 Tablespoons maple syrup
1/4 teaspoon ground cinnamon
Safflower Oil, to oil the squash skin

Heat the oven to 350°. Lightly oil the squash skin. Mix together the cooked quinoa, walnuts, cherries, syrup and cinnamon.

Stuff each squash half with the mixture. Cover the squash with foil wrap and place in a baking dish. Bake for 45 minutes or until the squash is tender when poked with a fork.

Remove the foil and gently mix some of the squash with the stuffing ingredients before placing on a serving platter.

QUINOA WITH CORN AND PUMPKIN SEEDS

1½ cups quinoa
3 cups water or vegetable broth
1/2 tsp. sea salt
1/4 tsp. freshly ground black pepper
1/3 cup raw pumpkin seeds
1 cup fresh or frozen cut corn kernels
2 tsp. olive oil
1/2 cup green onions, thinly sliced
2 tsp. garlic, minced
3/4 tsp. dried oregano
1/2 tsp. crushed red pepper flakes
1/4 cup chopped fresh cilantro or parsley

Place quinoa in a very fine-mesh strainer, and rinse well under running water for 1 minute.

In a medium saucepan over high heat, bring water, quinoa, salt, and black pepper to a boil. Cover, reduce heat to low, and simmer for 10 to 15 minutes or until quinoa is tender and all liquid is absorbed. Remove from heat.

Meanwhile, in a medium nonstick skillet over low heat, cook pumpkin seeds, stirring often, for 3 to 5 minutes or until lightly toasted and fragrant. Transfer toasted pumpkin seeds to a small bowl, and set aside.

Place corn and olive oil in the skillet, and sauté over medium heat, stirring often, for 2 minutes. Add green onions, garlic, oregano, and red pepper flakes, and sauté for 1 or 2 minutes or until green onions soften. Remove from heat.

Fluff quinoa with a fork to loosen grains. Add corn mixture, toasted pumpkin seeds, and cilantro, and stir gently with a fork to combine. Taste, adjust seasonings, and serve hot, cold, or at room temperature.

.

MOROCCAN STYLE VEGAN QUINOA

1 can (14 oz.) chickpeas, rinsed
3 small onions, quartered
1 cup carrots, cut in chunks
1 cup turnips, cut in chunks

Make stock by combining the following ingredients:
1/2 tsp. salt
2 garlic cloves
1 bay leaf
1/4 tsp. ground cumin
Pepper, to taste
2 Tbsp. olive oil
2 cups whole Brussels sprouts
2 cups water
1 Tbsp. olive oil
1 Tbsp. lemon or lime juice
2 cups quinoa

In a 3-qt. pot, place onions, carrots and turnips on top of the chickpeas and add enough water or stock to just cover vegetables. Add salt, garlic, bay, cumin, pepper and 2 Tbsp. olive oil.

Cover and bring to a boil. Reduce to light boil and cook for 40 minutes. Add Brussels sprouts and cook an additional 10 minutes. Adjust seasoning to taste.

While vegetables and chickpeas continue to cook, add 4 cups water and salt to a 2-qt. pot and bring to a boil. In a frying pan heat the remaining Tbsp. of oil. Add quinoa; stir quinoa continuously to toast (about 10 minutes).

Add to boiling stock, cover and simmer 15 to 20 minutes. Remove from heat. Allow to sit for 5 to 10 minutes. Gently mix vegetable/chickpea mixture. Cover pot, and allow to rest for another 5 to 10 minutes.

Serve by placing a large mound of quinoa on each individual plate. Flatten the mound in the center and fill with vegetables/chickpea mixture. Pour 1/2 c. of hot stock over all and serve hot.

Quinoa with Broccoli Rabe

1 cup quinoa
2 cups low sodium vegetable broth
2/3 cup chopped onion
1 tsp minced garlic
1 lb broccoli rabe, trimmed and chopped
¼ teaspoon salt
¼ teaspoon red pepper flakes

Toast quinoa, stirring, in nonstick skillet over medium-low heat, 5 minutes.

Bring broth and water to boil in medium saucepan; stir in quinoa.

Reduce heat to medium-low; cover and simmer 12 to 15 minutes until liquid is absorbed and quinoa is tender.

Fluff with fork and transfer to large bowl; cover and keep warm.

Heat a small amount of water or broth in large nonstick skillet over medium-high heat.

Add onion and garlic; cook 3 minutes. Stir in broccoli rabe, salt and red pepper. Cook until broccoli rabe is tender, 5 to 7 minutes. Stir vegetables into quinoa.

QUINOA WITH CARROTS & RAISINS

1 cup uncooked quinoa
1 1/3 cups fresh mushrooms, sliced
1/2 cup green onions, chopped
Lowfat cooking spray
2 3/4 cups water
1 1/2 teaspoons vegetable bouillon granules
1 teaspoon grated lemon rind
1/2 teaspoon dried thyme
1 cup shredded carrot
2 tablespoons raisins, chopped

Wash the Quinoa thoroughly to remove its bitter coating, drain and set aside.

Sauté mushrooms and green onions in a large nonstick skillet coated with cooking spray over medium-high heat for 5 minutes or until tender. Set aside.

Bring 2 3/4 cups water, bouillon cubes, lemon rind and thyme to a boil in a large saucepan. Add quinoa and carrot. Cook 10 to 15 minutes or until water is absorbed.

Stir in raisins and mushroom mixture.

QUINOA PILAF WITH RED AND YELLOW PEPPERS

1 oz minced shallots
1/2 oz minced garlic
1 1/2 pt Vegetable Stock
12 oz quinoa, rinsed
1/2 tsp kosher salt
1/4 tsp ground white pepper
1 bay leaf
1 sprig thyme
7 oz diced roasted red and yellow peppers

In a medium sauce pot, sweat the shallots and garlic in 2 tbsp of the stock until the shallots are translucent. Add the quinoa, remaining stock, salt, pepper, bay leaf, and thyme. Bring the liquid to a boil.

Cover the pot tightly and cook in a 350°F oven until the quinoa is tender and has absorbed all the liquid, about 15 minutes. Remove and discard the bay leaf and thyme. Fluff the quinoa with a fork to separate the grains and release steam. Fold in the peppers.

QUINOA PILAF, TOASTED

2 tablespoons finely chopped shallots or onion
6 cloves garlic, minced (1 tablespoon minced)
1 tablespoon extra-virgin olive oil
2 cups quinoa*, or barley, rinsed and well drained
3 cups vegetable broth
1 1/2 teaspoons chopped fresh thyme or 1/2 teaspoon dried thyme, crushed
1 bay leaf
1 cup bottled roasted red bell peppers, diced
Kosher salt
Freshly ground black pepper

In a large saucepan cook shallots and garlic in hot oil over medium heat until tender. Carefully stir in quinoa or barley. Cook and stir about 5 minutes or until quinoa or barley is golden brown.

Carefully stir in broth, thyme, and bay leaf Bring to boiling, reduce heat. Cover and simmer about 20 minutes or until quinoa is tender and fluffy (cook barley about 10 minutes or until tender and liquid is absorbed)

Discard bay leaf. Gently stir in roasted peppers. Season to taste with kosher salt and black pepper

QUINOA SUNCHOKE PILAF

3/4 cup quinoa
2 Tbsp olive oil
1/2 cup chopped onion
1 1/4 cup vegetable broth
1 cup chickpeas, cooked or canned, (drained and rinsed)
1 cup peeled, chopped sun chokes
1 cup peas, fresh or frozen
1 tsp pepper

Place the quinoa in a large bowl; fill with cold water.

Pour into a strainer, then return the quinoa to the bowl and rinse 4 times more. Drain well.

Heat the oil in a 2-quart saucepan over medium-high heat.

Add the rinsed quinoa and cook, stirring, until it cracks and pops, about 3 to 5 minutes. Add the onion and cook, stirring, until the onion is soft

Add the vegetable broth and bring to a boil over high heat. Add the chickpeas, sun chokes, peas, and pepper, and return to a boil.

Reduce the heat and simmer, covered, 20 minutes. Fluff with a fork. Serve.

Garlic-Toasted Quinoa with Vegetables

1 cup quinoa, rinsed
4 cloves garlic, diced
5 tablespoons olive oil
2 cups vegetable broth or water
1 bay leaf
1 bunch spinach or baby chard, rinsed and chopped
1 bunch asparagus, washed and chopped, with woody ends removed
10 shiitake mushrooms, sliced
1/4 cup slivered almonds
1 tablespoon soy sauce

Sauté garlic in 2 tablespoons oil in a large pot over high heat for 2 minutes or until tender. Add quinoa and another tablespoon of oil to coat the quinoa.

Reduce heat to medium and toast, stirring constantly, until the quinoa turns brown (about 10 minutes).

Add the broth or water and bay leaf, and bring to a boil. Reduce heat, cover and simmer for 15 minutes (until liquid is absorbed).

While the quinoa is cooking, sauté the mushrooms in remaining 2 tablespoons of oil until soft. Add asparagus and cook until just tender. Add the greens and cook until wilted. Remove bay leaf and add the mushroom and greens to the quinoa. Add the almonds, and stir well to combine. Season with the soy sauce.

Quinoa Carrot Zucchini Casserole Recipe

1 c quinoa
1/4 cup dried currants
1/4 cup sunflower seeds
1 or 2 bay leaves
1 cinnamon stick
2 Tbs olive oil
1 c. celery, chopped small
2 medium carrots
2 small zucchini
1 tsp ground coriander
1/2 tsp paprika
pinch cayenne
1/2 tsp dried ginger
1/2 tsp ground cumin
1/2 tsp rock salt
1 1/2 - 1 3/4 cup boiling water or vegetable stock
Note: Use smaller amount of water for slow cooker or crockpot
1/4 c. minced parsley or cilantro
fresh ground pepper to taste

Soak quinoa 15 minutes to an hour, rinse three times through a fine metal strainer, leave to drain

Heat olive oil on medium in a large sauté pan or frying pan. Chop celery in small pieces. Peel and chop carrots in 1/2" dice

Wash, trim, and chop zucchini in 1 " dice. Stir fry celery until transparent. Add carrots, stir fry five minutes. Add zucchini, stir fry one minute

Add the spices, except for the fresh herb and salt, lower heat and stir until they start to brown. Preheat oven to 350 degrees. Use a three or four quart oven proof casserole with lid. Add all ingredients except fresh herb and pepper. Stir in 1 3/4 cups boiling water or stock, cover, and bake 20 minutes, or until all the water is absorbed

Before serving, remove the bay leaves and cinnamon stick. Stir in the minced fresh parsley or cilantro, fresh ground pepper, and serve.

Quinoa Tofu & Veggie Casserole Recipe

1 c quinoa
1/2 lb extra firm tofu
1/4 cup cashew pieces
1 Tbsp peeled minced fresh ginger
1 garlic clove, minced
1/4 cup chopped black olives
1 six inch zucchini
1 medium carrot
2 stalks celery
1 bay leaf
1/4 tsp dried rosemary leaf
1 tsp dried basil leaf
1 tsp coriander
1/2 tsp powdered fennel
2 - 3 Tbsp olive oil
1/2 tsp garlic salt
1 Tbsp soy sauce
1 3/4 cup water
1/2 tsp salt
1/4 c. minced parsley or cilantro

Soak quinoa 15 - 20 minutes, rinse, drain and set aside

Cut tofu in bite sized cubes, place in a small bowl, sprinkle with garlic salt and soy sauce and shake or stir to coat with marinade. Set aside Heat 1 -2 Tbsp olive oil on low in a large sauté pan or shallow 4 qt sauce pan Mince ginger and garlic Chop celery in small pieces Peel and chop carrots in 1/2" dice Wash, trim, and chop zucchini in 1 " dice

Coarsely chop olives and set aside Turn the heat up to medium, and stir fry ginger, garlic, celery, carrots for 5 minutes Add zucchini and stir fry another five minutes Stir in dry spices, herbs Add the drained quinoa and stir until coated with spices Add 1 3/4 cup water, and salt, then bring to a boil, cover and cook 15 minutes on low

Meanwhile, fry the tofu cubes on medium, stirring and turning, until browned Stir tofu, chopped olives and parsley into the quinoa and veg Heat on low for another few minutes and serve

Quinoa Stuffed Portobello Mushroom Recipe

1 large Portobello mushroom per person
Olive oil
Balsamic vinegar
Sea salt and ground pepper, to taste

For the stuffing:
Chopped fresh garlic, to taste
About 1/3 to 1/2 cup of cooked quinoa per mushroom cap
A handful of yellow and red grape or cherry tomatoes, halved or quartered depending upon size
1 scallion (spring onion) per person, sliced
A sprinkle of raisins
A sprinkle of toasted pine nuts
Sea salt and ground pepper, to taste
Fresh chopped parsley, basil or mint

Preheat the oven to 350 degrees F. Lightly oil the bottom of a baking or gratin dish. Gently clean off the mushroom caps; slice off the stems and using a sharp teaspoon carefully scrape out the gills. Place the caps in the baking dish.

Drizzle with a scant amount of olive oil and a touch of balsamic vinegar. Season with a little sea salt and pepper. Pre-bake the mushrooms for 12 to 15 minutes to soften a bit. In a skillet, heat a little olive oil and toss in the garlic.

Stir for a minute. Add in the cooked quinoa, tomatoes, scallions, raisins, pine nuts. Season to taste with sea salt and ground pepper. Stir to combine. Add more olive oil to moisten, if needed. Gently heat through, briefly.

Remove from heat. Add in the fresh chopped herbs. Stuff each mushroom cap. Tent with foil. Bake in the oven for 15 to 20 minutes, till the mushroom cap is tender. You can also assemble these ahead of

Quinoa with Herbs and Mixed Olives

2 tablespoons extra-virgin olive oil
1 small onion, finely chopped
1 clove garlic, finely chopped
1 1/2 cups quinoa, well rinsed
Salt
1/2 cup pitted and thinly sliced black and green olives
1/2 cup pine nuts, toasted
1/3 cup fresh basil leaves, finely chopped
1/3 cup cilantro leaves, finely chopped
1/3 cup flat-leaf parsley leaves, finely chopped

Rinse quinoa at least 3 times to remove its bitter resin.

In a large saucepan or deep skillet, heat the olive oil over medium heat. Add the onion and cook, stirring often, until softened, about 3 minutes. Add the garlic and cook just until fragrant, about 30 seconds. Add the quinoa and cook, stirring, for 1 minute.

Stir in 2 1/4 cups water, season with salt and bring to a boil over high heat. Lower the heat, cover and simmer until the water is absorbed, about 15 minutes. Let stand for 5 minutes. Add the olives, pine nuts, basil, cilantro and parsley and toss with a fork to combine; season with salt

Butternut squash chili with quinoa

1 large onion , finely chopped
2 garlic cloves , crushed
olive oil
1 tbsp mild chili powder
1 butternut squash , about 1kg, peeled and cubed
100g quinoa , soaked in cold water for 10 minutes 2 x 400g tins chopped tomatoes
400g tin red kidney beans
a small bunch coriander , chopped

Cook the onion and garlic in 1 tbsp olive oil until soft (about 7 minutes). Add the chili powder, cook for a minute then add the squash, quinoa and tomatoes.

Simmer for 10-15 minutes until the squash and quinoa are tender and the sauce has thickened. Add the beans and heat through. Stir in the coriander and serve in bowls.

Tofu, Asparagus, and Red Pepper Stir-Fry with Quinoa

DRESSING:
2 tablespoons rice vinegar
2 tablespoons low-sodium soy sauce
2 teaspoons dark sesame oil
Dash of crushed red pepper

STIR-FRY:
1 1/2 cups water
1 1/2 cups uncooked quinoa
1 tablespoon dark sesame oil
1 cup chopped onion
2 garlic cloves, minced
2 cups red bell pepper strips
2 cups sliced mushrooms
2 cups (1-inch) sliced asparagus (about 1 pound)
1/2 teaspoon salt
1 (12.3-ounce) package reduced-fat firm tofu, drained and cubed
2 tablespoons sesame seeds

To prepare dressing, combine first 4 ingredients in a small bowl; stir with a whisk. Set aside.

To prepare stir-fry, bring water to a boil in a small saucepan. Stir in the quinoa; cover, reduce heat, and simmer 10 minutes. Remove from heat. Let stand, covered, 10 minutes; fluff with a fork.

Heat 1 tablespoon oil in a large nonstick skillet over medium-high heat. Add onion and garlic, and stir-fry 5 minutes. Add the bell pepper, mushrooms, asparagus, salt, and tofu; stir-fry 3 minutes. Stir in dressing. Serve over quinoa, and sprinkle with sesame seeds.

Vegetable Quinoa Bake

1 md Yellow onion; chopped
1/2 tsp Salt
1 Tbs Canola oil
1 lg Green or red bell pepper;
1 1/2 Tbs Dried parsley
1/2 tsp Black pepper
1 sm Zucchini; diced
2 c Peeled & diced butternut
2 Cloves garlic; minced
1 c Chopped kale; spinach or
8 md Button mushrooms; sliced
1 1/2 c Quinoa; rinsed and drained
1 c Peeled & diced carrot
1 Jalapeno pepper (optional);
3 c Water

PREHEAT oven to 400F/200C. In a large saucepan, heat the oil. Add the onion, mushrooms, bell pepper, jalapeno pepper, if desired, zucchini, and garlic and sauté for about 5 to 7 minutes.

Stir in the water, quinoa, squash, carrots kale, and seasonings and bring to a boil. Transfer the mixture to a 9" X 13" casserole dish and cover. Bake for 30 to 40 minutes, until all of the liquid is absorbed.

Remove from the oven and fluff with a fork. Let stand for 5 minutes before serving. Makes 6 to 8 servings.

Quinoa with Eggplant

1 large eggplant
2 tablespoons olive oil
1 large onion, chopped
3 cloves garlic, minced
3 ounces tomato paste (1/2 of a small can or tube)
1/2 teaspoon ground cumin
1/2 teaspoon ground coriander
1/2 teaspoon allspice
pinch cayenne pepper, or to taste
1 16-ounce can chickpeas, undrained
2 tablespoons pinenuts
3 cups cooked quinoa

Optional garnishes
lemon wedges
chopped Italian parsley
freshly ground pepper and salt to taste

Select a shiny, firm eggplant. Cut off the stem end. Pierce the skin in several places with a sharp knife. Set the plate on a microwave-safe dish and cook it on high for 7-10 minutes, or until it collapses. (Time varies depending on the strength of your microwave). When it is cool enough to handle, cut it into small pieces.

Meanwhile, heat the olive oil in a large pot. Stir in the onions and garlic and cook until softened, about 5 minutes. Stir in the tomato paste and spices and continue to cook, stirring occasionally, until the eggplant is ready. Add the eggplant, chickpeas, pinenuts and quinoa and cook 5 minutes more. If desired, sprinkle wih chopped parsley and pass the lemon wedges, salt and pepper.

Chapter 6 - Vegan Quinoa Desserts

Nectarine Pie with Quinoa Walnut Crust

CRUST
1 1/2 cups Quinoa
1 cup walnuts
1/2 teaspoon Sea Salt
3 Tablespoons Extra Virgin Olive Oil
1/2 cup Vanilla Soymilk
2 Tablespoons maple syrup

FILLING
5 cups nectarines or peaches, sliced, (about 7 medium)
1 1/2 cups Apple Juice
1 pinch Sea Salt
3 Tablespoons Kuzu Root Starch, dissolved in 1/4 cup cold water

Directions

Preheat oven to 350°. Place quinoa in a blender and grind about 5 minutes until it becomes fine flour or grind in a flour mill. Remove and place in a mixing bowl. Coarsely grind the walnuts in the blender and place in the bowl. Add sea salt, mix, and add the oil, Soymilk and maple syrup. Mix thoroughly. Press the dough evenly into a 9" pie plate to form the crust. Pre-bake the crust for 10 minutes.

While the crust is baking, place the nectarines, juice and sea salt in a medium saucepan and bring to a boil. Reduce the flame to low and slowly add the dissolved kuzu, stirring constantly to prevent lumping. When thick, about 1 minute or so, pour the filling into the pre-baked crust. Bake another 10 minutes until the crust is golden brown. Remove and cool before slicing.

Quinoa Pudding

1 cup quinoa
2 cups water
2 cups apple juice
1 cup raisins
2 tablespoons lemon juice
1 teaspoon ground cinnamon, or to taste
salt to taste
2 teaspoons vanilla extract

Place quinoa in a sieve and rinse thoroughly. Allow to drain, then place quinoa in a medium saucepan with water. Bring to a boil over high heat. Cover pan with lid, lower heat, and allow to simmer until all water is absorbed and quinoa is tender, about 15 minutes.

Mix in apple juice, raisins, lemon juice, cinnamon, and salt. Cover pan and allow to simmer for 15 minutes longer. Stir in vanilla extract. Serve warm.

Creamy Quinoa Pudding

1 cup Quinoa, rinsed
2 1/2 cups Soymilk
1/8 teaspoon Sea Salt
1 teaspoon sesame butter or sesame tahini
2 Tablespoons Barley Malt Syrup or maple syrup
2 Tablespoons Kuzu Root Starch, dissolved in 3 T. cold water
1 Tablespoon pure vanilla extract
1/2 teaspoon nutmeg, freshly grated or ground cinnamon

Directions

Put quinoa, Soymilk, and salt in a saucepan and bring to a boil. Cover and simmer for 20 minutes. Add sesame butter and barley malt syrup. Mix well. Add kuzu, stirring constantly until mixture thickens. Add vanilla and spices. Top with your choice of chopped nuts, roasted seeds or fruit. Delicious warm or chilled.

Quinoa Fruit Pudding

1 cup Quinoa, washed and drained
2 cups water
1/8 teaspoon Sea Salt
1 teaspoon ground cinnamon
1/3 cup maple syrup
2 cups soy milk
1/3 cup apples, diced
1/4 cup Dried Wild Blueberries or Dried Cranberries
1 teaspoon pure vanilla extract

Place the quinoa, water, sea salt and cinnamon in a medium saucepan. Cover and bring to a boil. Reduce the flame and simmer for 15 minutes. Add the soymilk, and maple syrup. Simmer uncovered for 10 minutes. Add the apples and cook for 2 to 3 minutes. Turn off the flame and mix in the blueberries and vanilla. Cover and let sit for 15 minutes to thicken.

Quinoa Cherry Pudding

1 cup Quinoa, washed and drained
2 cups water
1/8 teaspoon Sea Salt
1/3 cup Dried Cherries, coarsely chopped or Dried Wild Blueberries or Dried Cranberries, do not chop
1 teaspoon ground cinnamon
1/3 cup maple syrup
2 cups soymilk
1 teaspoon pure vanilla extract
1/3 cup slivered almonds, dry pan roasted for garnish or Roasted Almonds, chopped

Place the quinoa, water, sea salt, dried cherries and cinnamon in a medium saucepan. Cover and bring to a boil. Reduce the flame and simmer for 15 minutes. Add the soymilk and syrup. Simmer, uncovered, for another 10 minutes. Turn off the flame and mix in the vanilla. Cover the pan and let sit for 15 minutes to thicken. Place in serving bowls and garnish with slivered almonds.

Quinoa Chocolate Brownies

Preheat the oven to 350 degrees F. Line an 11x13-inch baking pan with lightly greased parchment.

In a mixing bowl, whisk together the dry ingredients:

1 cup sorghum flour
1 cup Quinoa Flakes
1/3 cup Quinoa Flour or buckwheat flour
1/2 cup potato starch
1/4 cup cocoa powder
1 teaspoon xanthan gum
1 teaspoon sea salt
1 teaspoon baking soda
2 teaspoons baking powder
1 teaspoon cinnamon
1 2/3 cups organic light brown sugar

Add in:
2/3 cup light olive oil
3 tablespoons pure maple syrup
1/2 teaspoon Vanilla Powder or 1 tablespoon bourbon vanilla extract

Combine the wet and dry ingredients and beat with a stand mixer, or your own elbow grease- with a sturdy wooden spoon- until you get a sticky batter.

Make your egg replacement:
1 tablespoon Egg Replacer
4 tablespoons warm water

Whip the egg replacer ingredients till foamy and frothy. [If you are adding eggs instead, beat two large free-range organic eggs; and omit the egg replacement formula.] Add the egg replacer to the batter and combine well. The dough should be thick and rather sticky.

Add: 2 to 4 tablespoons of warm water, as needed to achieve a dough that sticks together when you pinch it- much like a soft cookie dough. (Three tablespoons of warm water worked for us.)Now add in 1/2 cup dairy-free chocolate chips or chopped nuts, as you prefer (or both!)

Stir to combine. Spread the batter into the prepared baking pan, and using wet or oiled hands, press and smooth the surface evenly. Place the pan into the center of a pre-heated oven and bake until set - about 25 to 35 minutes depending upon your oven and altitude.

Insert s thin knife to check if you are unsure to make certain the center has baked thoroughly. Cool on a wire rack. Using a thin sharp knife, cut the brownies into squares; wrap them in foil; bag in a freezer storage bag. Freeze. Delicious warm or slightly chilled. Makes 15 to 18 brownies.

Apple-Quinoa Cake

2 whole medium apples, cored and coarsely grated (about 1 cup lightly packed or 200 g.)–I used Macintosh and left the skins on
1/2 cup (125 ml.) agave nectar
1/2 cup (125 ml.) sunflower or other light-tasting oil
2 cups (160 g.) cooked quinoa
2 tsp. (10 ml.) finely ground chia seeds*
2 tsp. (10 ml.) pure vanilla extract
1 tsp. (5 ml.) apple cider vinegar
1/4 cup (40 g.) sunflower seeds
1/4 cup raisins
1-1/3 cups (160 g.) whole oat flour
1 tsp. (5 ml.) baking powder
1/2 tsp. (2.5 ml.) baking soda
1 tsp. (5 ml.) ground ginger
2 tsp. (10 ml.) ground cinnamon
1 tsp. (10 ml.) or less, to taste, cardamom
1/2 tsp. (2.5 ml.) sea salt
1/4 cup whole oats

Preheat oven to 350F (180C). Grease a 9? square pan, or line with parchment paper.

In a medium bowl, mix the grated apple, agave nectar, oil, quinoa, Saba, vanilla, vinegar, sunflower seeds and raisins. Set aside.

In a large bowl, sift the flour, baking powder, soda, ginger, cinnamon, cardamom, and sea salt. Add the oats. Add the wet mixture to the dry and mix well.

Pour into prepared pan and smooth the top. Bake for 30-40 minutes, until a tester inserted in the center comes out clean. Allow to cool before cutting into slices.

Gluten Free Quinoa Peanut Butter Cookie Recipe

Group 1:
1/3 cup Brown Rice Flour
1/3 cup Sorghum Flour
1/3 cup cornstarch
1 cup quinoa flakes
1 tsp baking powder
1/2 tsp salt

Group 2:
3/8 cup canola oil
3/8 cups peanut butter
1/2 cup sugar
1/2 cup brown sugar
1/4 cup vanilla rice milk
1 tsp vanilla extract

Preheat oven to 350 F and spray one cookie sheet with nonstick cooking spray.

Combine dry ingredients (group 1) thoroughly in one medium bowl and mix wet ingredients (group 2) in one large bowl. Add the dry ingredients to the large bowl and mix to form dough.

To make monster cookies, fill 1/3 cup measuring cup with dough, roll it into a ball and then flatten on cookie sheet. To make normal cookies, use 1-2 tablespoon balls of dough. Bake monster cookies for 12-15 minutes or until they seem to be dry and slightly golden. Let cool on cookie sheet for at least 10 minutes or they will fall apart when you try to take them off the sheet.

The normal cookies bake for 8-10 minutes and should probably cool on the sheet for at least 5 minutes before removal. In both cases use a good metal spatula to get the cookies off the sheet.